Daniel B. Towner, B. F. Mills

Selections from Hymns New and Old

with standard hymns designed especially for use in meetings

Daniel B. Towner, B. F. Mills

Selections from Hymns New and Old

with standard hymns designed especially for use in meetings

ISBN/EAN: 9783337831028

Printed in Europe, USA, Canada, Australia, Japan

Cover: Foto ©Lupo / pixelio.de

More available books at **www.hansebooks.com**

INDEX.

A charge to keep I have	113
Acquaint thyself quickly	135
Alas! and did my Saviour	13
All hail the power of Jesus name	31
All people that on earth	6
Amazing grace! how sweet the sound	83
Am I a soldier	72
Anywhere with Jesus	15
Behold! what love	30
Blessed assurance	27
Blessed be the fountain	5
Blest be the tie	48
Christ of all my hopes	108
Come, every pious heart	44
Come, Holy Ghost	63
Come, Holy Spirit	73
Come, let us join	110
Come, my soul, thy suit prepare	88
Come, Spirit, come	46
Come, Thou Almighty King	62
Come, thou fount	74
Come to Jesus	76
Come unto Me	141
Come we that love	57
Come, ye disconsolate	142
Come, ye sinners	132
Delay not, delay not	136
Depth of mercy	144
Fade, fade, each earthly	146
From mountain top	71
From the cross uplifted high	26
Glory be to the Father	1
God be with you	53
God calling yet	101
Guide me, O, Thou Great Jehovah	2
Hail! my ever Blessed Jesus	68
Hark! my soul	105
Hasten, sinner	104
How firm a foundation	138
How gentle God's command	50
How shall the young	112
Holy Ghost, dispel our sadness	67
Holy Ghost, with light divine	87
Holy, Holy, Holy Lord God	54
I gave my life for thee	12
I have a Savior	128
I have found a friend	16
I have work enough	8
I hear thy welcome voice	38
I know not why God's	41
I love to tell the story	14
I love Thy kingdom	115
I once was a stranger	140
I saw a way-worn traveler	58
In the Rock of Ages hiding	9
In heavenly love abiding	98
I've reached the land	96
Jesus engraved on my heart	36
Jesus is pleading with my poor soul	66
Jesus is tenderly calling for thee	65
Jesus, I my cross	131
Jesus, lover of my soul	130
Jesus, my Lord, to Thee I cry	92
Jesus, my Savior	51
Jesus shall reign	118
Joy to the world, the Lord	56
Just as I am	124
Look, ye saints, the sight is glorious	60
Lord, I hear of showers	84
Lord, I am Thine	117
Lord Jesus, I long	93
Lord of the worlds	45
Lor l, we come before Thee now	86
Love divine, all love	133
Majestic sweetness sits enthroned	80
'Mid scenes of confusion	151
More love to Thee	39
Move forward	40
Must I go and empty handed	15
Must Jesus bear the cross alone	95
My faith looks up	123
My Father is rich	18
My hope is built	81
My God, my Father	126
My Jesus, I love Thee	47
My Soul be on thy guard	114
Nearer my God to thee	29
Now I resolve	120
Now is the accepted	116
O, could I speak	91
O, do not let the word	94
O for a closer walk	111
O for a heart	121
O for a faith	122
O, for a shout of joy	43
O for a thousand tongues	32
O happy day	127
O Holy Spirit, come	148
O Lord, Thy work revive	149
O, love divine, how sweet	90
O, scatter seeds of loving deeds	10
O, think of the home over there	79
O turn ye	134
O, where shall rest be found	49
O, who are these so near	42
Once more, my soul	64
Onward, Christian soldiers	37
Our Lord is now rejected	28
Our Master has taken His journey	20
Pardon in Jesus my brother	85
People of the living God	107
Quiet, Lord, my wayward heart	25
Rock of Ages cleft for me	24
Salvation, O the joyful	109
Saviour, I follow on	147
Saviour, visit Thy plantation	70
Sing them over again to me	4
Sinners Jesus will receive	10
Sinners, turn, why will	129
So let our lips and lives	119
Sowing in the morning	60
Soul of mine	143
Stand up, stand up	99
Sun of My Soul	34
Sweet hour of prayer	82
Take my life	106
The Great Physician	97
The Lord is my Shepherd	139
The Lord my pasture shall	3
The voice of free grace	52
There are angels hovering 'round	77
There is a fountain	103
There shall be showers	23
There's a land that is fairer	78
There's a stranger	33
Thou art my God	89
'Tis grace, 'tis grace	55
To-day the Saviour	137
To-day Thy mercy calls	100
To Thee who from the narrow road	22
We praise Thee, O God	11
What a friend we have in Jesus	75
What means this eager, anxious throng	61
When I survey the wondrous cross	102
When we walk with the Lord	59
While Jesus whispers	7
While Thee I seek	150
Who is on the Lord's side	19
Why will ye waste	35
With tearful eyes	125
Yield not to temptation	145

HYMNS NEW AND OLD.

No. 1.   Gloria Patri.

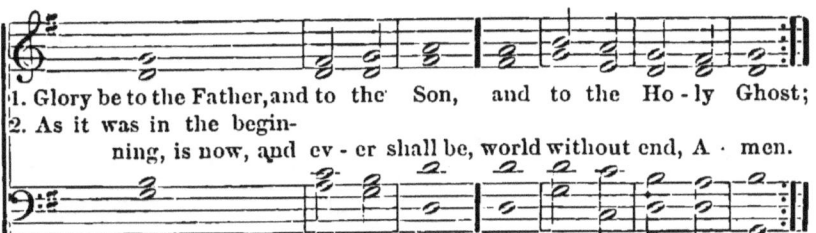

1. Glory be to the Father, and to the Son, and to the Ho-ly Ghost;
2. As it was in the beginning, is now, and ev-er shall be, world without end, A-men.

No. 2.   Guide Me.

"For Thy name's sake, lead me, and guide me."—Psalm 31: 3.

Rev. W. Williams.   Wm. L. Viner.

1. Guide me, O Thou great Jeho-vah, Pilgrim thro' this barren land:
D.C.—Bread of heaven, Bread of hea-ven, Feed me till I want no more.

2. O-pen now the crystal fountain, Whence the healing waters flow;
D.C.—Strong Deliv'rer, Strong Deliv'rer, Be Thou still my strength and shield.

3. When I tread the verge of Jor-dan, Bid my anxious fears subside;
D.C.—Songs of prais-es, Songs of prais-es, I will ev-er give to Thee.

I am weak, but Thou art mighty, Hold me with Thy powerful hand:
Let the fie-ry cloud-y pil-lar Lead me all my journey through:
Bear me thro' the swelling current, Land me safe on Canaan's side:

No. 3. The Lord my Pasture shall Prepare.

The Lord is my Shepherd.—Ps. 23: 1.

Arranged from HAYDN.

1. The Lord my pas-ture shall pre-pare, And feed me with a shepherd's care; His pres-ence shall my wants sup-ply, And guard me with a watch-ful eye; My noon-day walks He shall at-tend, And all my mid-night hours defend.
2. When in the sul-try glebe I faint, Or on the thirs-ty mountain pant, To fer-tile vales and dew-y meads, My wea-ry, wan-d'ring steps He leads, Where peace-ful riv-ers, soft and slow, A-mid the ver-dant landscape flow.
3. Though in a bare and rug-ged way, Thro' de-vious lone-ly wilds I stray, Thy boun-ty shall my pains be-guile; The bar-ren wil-der-ness shall smile, With sud-den greens and herb-age crown'd, And streams shall murmur all a-round.
4. Though in the paths of death I tread, With gloomy hor-rors o-ver-spread, My stead-fast heart shall fear no ill, For Thou, O Lord, art with me still; Thy friend-ly crook shall give me aid, And guide me through the dreadful shade.

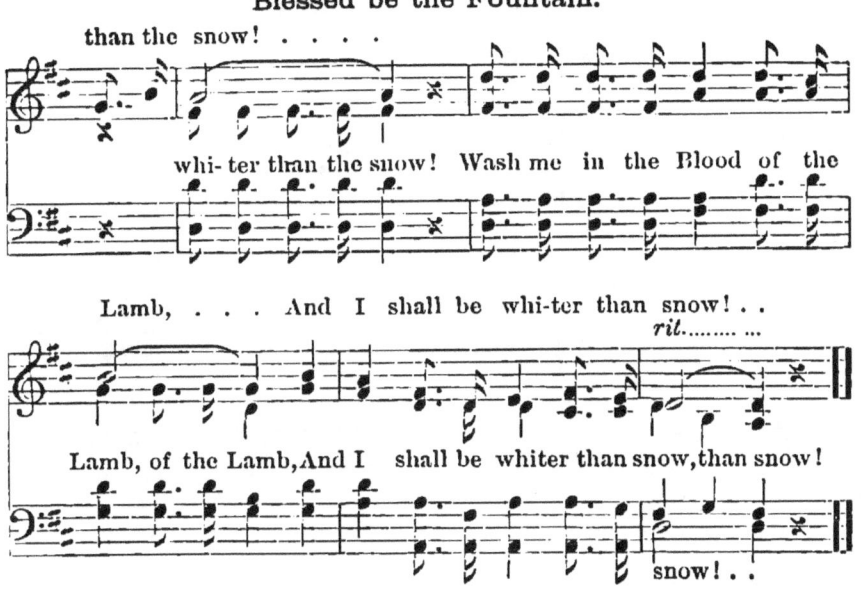

No. 6. Old Hundred. L. M.

"Come before His presence with singing."—Psa. 100: 2.

Rev. WM. KETHE, 1561.   G. FRANC, 1545.

1. All people that on earth do dwell, Sing to the Lord with cheerful voice;
2. Know that the Lord is God indeed; Without our aid He did us make:
3. O enter then His gates with praise, Approach with joy His courts unto:

Him serve with mirth, His praise forth tell, Come ye before Him and rejoice.
We are His flock, He doth us feed, And for His sheep He doth us take.
Praise, laud, and bless His name always, For it is seem-ly so to do.

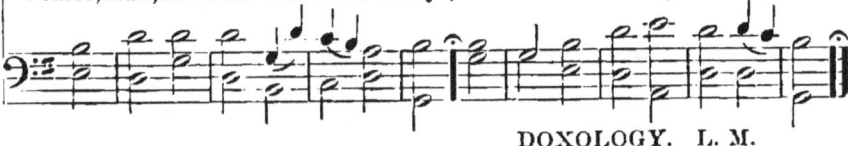

DOXOLOGY. L. M.

4 For why? the Lord our God is good,   Praise God, from whom all blessings
    His mercy is forever sure;   flow;
   His truth at all times firmly stood,   Praise Him, all creatures here below·
   And shall from age to age endure.   Praise Him above, ye heavenly host;
                                      Praise Father, Son, and Holy Ghost.
                                                         BP. THOS. KEN. 1697.

No. 11. Revive us Again.

"*O Lord, revive Thy work.*" — Hab. 3: 2.

Rev. WM. PATON MACKAY, 1866.   ENGLISH MELODY.

1. We praise Thee, O God! for the Son of Thy love, For Jesus who died, and is now gone above.
2. We praise Thee, O God! for Thy Spri-it of light, Who has shown us our Saviour, and scattered our night.
3. All glo-ry and praise to the Lamb that was slain, Who has borne all our sins, and hath cleansed every stain.
4. All glo-ry and praise to the God of all grace, Who has bought us, and sought us, and guided our ways.
5. Re-vive us a-gain; fill each heart with Thy love; May each soul be re-kindled with fire from a-bove.

CHORUS.

Hal-le-lu-jah, Thine the glo-ry, Hal-le-lu-jah! a-men; Hal-lelu-jah! Thine the glory, revive us a-gain.

No. 12.

Key C.   Tune, — No. 21, G. H.

1 I gave my life for thee,
   My precious blood I shed
  That thou might'st ransomed be,
   And quickened from the dead.
‖: I gave, I gave my life for thee, :‖
  What hast thou given for Me.

2 My Father's house of light,
   My glory-circled throne
  I left, for earthly night,
   For wand'rings sad and lone.
‖: I left, I left it all for thee,: ‖
  Hast thou left aught for Me?

3 I suffered much for thee,
   More than thy tongue can tell,
  Of bitterest agony,
   To rescue thee from hell;
‖: I've borne, I've borne it all for thee,: ‖
  What hast thou borne for Me?

4 And I have brought to thee,
   Down from My home above,
  Salvation full and free,
   My pardon and My love;
‖: I bring, I bring rich gifts to thee,: ‖
  What hast thou brought to Me?

FRANCES R. HAVERGAL.

No. 13. At the Cross.

The blood of Jesus Christ His Son cleanseth us from all sin.—1 John 1: 7.

R. E. HUDSON.

1. A-las! and did my Saviour bleed, And did my Sovereign die,
2. Was it for crimes that I have done, He groan'd upon the tree?
3. But drops of grief can ne'er re-pay, The debt of love I owe;

Would He de-vote that sa-cred head For such a worm as I?
A-maz-ing pit-y, grace unknown, And love beyond de-gree!
Here, Lord, I give my-self a-way, 'Tis all that I can do!

CHORUS.

At the cross, at the cross, where I first saw the light, And the bur-den of my heart roll'd away— rolled away, It was there by faith I received my sight, And now I am hap-py all the day.

Copyright, 1885, by R. E. HUDSON.

No. 14. I Love to Tell the Story.

"I will speak of Thy wondrous work."—Ps. 145: 5.

Miss KATE HANKEY, 1867. W. G. FISCHER. By per.

1. I love to tell the Sto-ry Of unseen things above, Of Jesus and His Glo-ry Of Je-sus and His Love! I love to tell the Sto-ry! Be-cause I know it's true; It sat-is-fies my longings, As nothing else could do.
2. I love to tell the Sto-ry! More wonderful it seems, Than all the golden fan-cies Of all our golden dreams. I love to tell the Sto-ry! It did so much for me! And that is just the reason, I tell it now to thee.
3. I love to tell the Sto-ry! 'Tis pleasant to repeat What seems, each time I tell it, More won-der-ful-ly sweet. I love to tell the Sto-ry; For some have never heard The message of salvation From God's own Holy Word.
4. I love to tell the Sto-ry! For those who know it best Seem hungering and thirsting To hear it, like the rest. And when, in scenes of glory, I sing the new, new song, 'Twill be—the old, old story That I have loved so long.

CHORUS.

I love to tell the Sto-ry! 'Twill be my theme in glo-ry,

I Love to Tell the Story.

To tell the Old, Old Sto - ry   Of   Je - sus and   His love.

No. 15. Must I Go and Empty-Handed?

C. C. LUTHER.　　　　　(DAN. 12: 3.)　　　　GEO. C. STEBBINS. By per.

After a month only of Christian life, nearly all of it upon a sick bed, a young man of nearly 30 years lay dying. Suddenly a look of sadness crossed his face, and to the query of a friend he exclaimed, "No, I am not afraid, Jesus saves me now; but oh, *must I go and empty-handed?*"

DUET.

1. "Must I   go and emp - ty-hand-ed," Thus my dear Redeemer meet?
2. Not at death I shrink nor fal - ter, For my Saviour saves me now;
3. Oh, the years of sin - ning wast-ed, Could I but re - call them now,
4. Oh, ye saints, a-rouse, be ear - nest, Up and work while yet 'tis day,

Not one day   of ser - vice give Him, Lay no tro - phy at His feet.
But to meet Him emp-ty-hand - ed, Tho't of that now clouds my brow.
I   would give them to my Sav - iour, To   His will I'd glad-ly bow.
Ere the night of death o'ertakes thee, Strive for souls while still you may.

CHORUS.

"Must I   go and emp - ty-hand-ed," Must I meet my Sav- iour so?

Not one soul with which to greet Him, Must I emp-ty-hand - ed go?

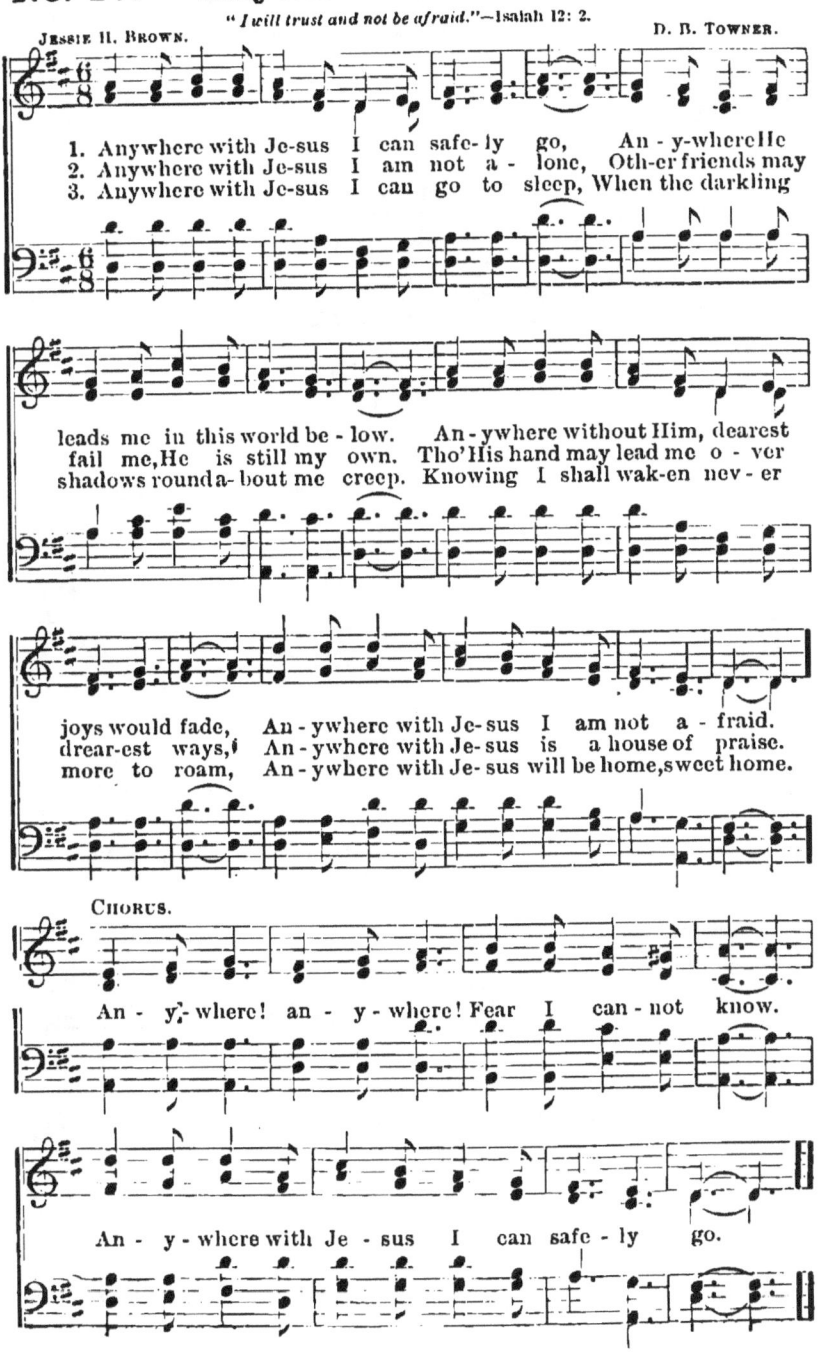

No. 18. The Child of a King.

Let the children of Zion be joyful in their King.—Ps. 149: 2.

HATTIE E. BUELL. Rev. JOHN B. SUMNER.

1. My Father is rich in houses and lands, He holdeth the wealth of the world in His hands; Of rubies and diamonds, of sil-ver and gold, His coffers are full, He has rich-es untold.
2. My Father's own Son, the Saviour of men! Once wandered o'er earth as the poor-est of them; But now He is reigning for-ev-er on high, And will give us a home in the sweet by and by.
3. I once was an outcast stranger on earth, A sin-ner by choice, an "a-lien" by birth; But I've been "adopted," my name's written down An heir to a mansion, a robe, and a crown.
4. A tent or a cottage, why should I care? They're building a palace for me o-ver there; Tho' exiled from home, yet still I may sing, All glo-ry to God, I'm the child of a King.

CHORUS.

I'm the child of a King, the child of a King; With Jesus, my Saviour, I'm the child of a King.

By permission.

No. 21. Seeds of Promise.

JESSIE H. BROWN.   FRED. A. FILLMORE. By per.

1. Oh, scatter seeds of lov-ing deeds, Along the fer-tile field, For
2. Tho' sown in tears thro' weary years, The seed will surely live; Tho'
3. The harvest-home of God will come, And af-ter toil and care; With

grain will grow from what you sow, And fruitful harvest yield.
great the cost it is not lost, For God will fruitage give.
joy untold your sheaves of gold Will all be garnered there.

CHORUS.

Then day by day . . . . along your way, ... The seeds of prom - - - ise

Then day by day   a-long your way,   The seeds of promise cast, the

cast, ... That ripened grain . . . . . from hill and

seeds of promise cast,   That ripened grain

plain, ... Be gathered home . . . . at last. . . . . .

from hill and plain,   Be gathered home at last, be gathered home at last.

Be gathered home at last. . . . .

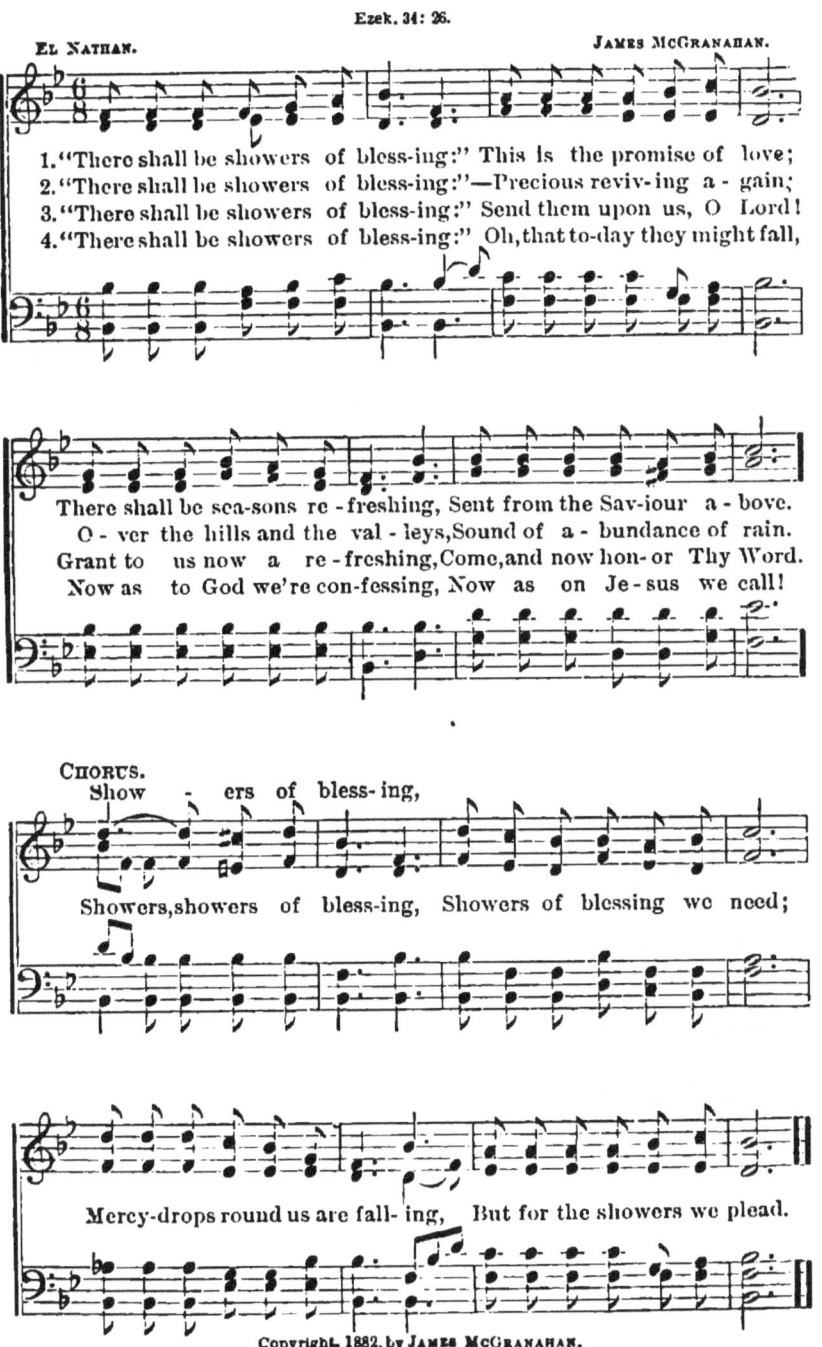

No. 23. There shall be Showers of Blessings.

Ezek. 34: 26.

EL NATHAN.   JAMES McGRANAHAN.

1. "There shall be showers of bless-ing:" This is the promise of love;
2. "There shall be showers of bless-ing:"—Precious reviv-ing a-gain;
3. "There shall be showers of bless-ing:" Send them upon us, O Lord!
4. "There shall be showers of bless-ing:" Oh, that to-day they might fall,

There shall be sea-sons re-freshing, Sent from the Sav-iour a-bove.
O-ver the hills and the val-leys, Sound of a-bundance of rain.
Grant to us now a re-freshing, Come, and now hon-or Thy Word.
Now as to God we're con-fessing, Now as on Je-sus we call!

CHORUS.
Show - ers of bless-ing,
Showers, showers of bless-ing, Showers of blessing we need;
Mercy-drops round us are fall-ing, But for the showers we plead.

Copyright, 1882, by JAMES McGRANAHAN.

No. 24. Rock of Ages.

A. TOPLADY. Tune, TOPLADY. 6 lines, 7s.

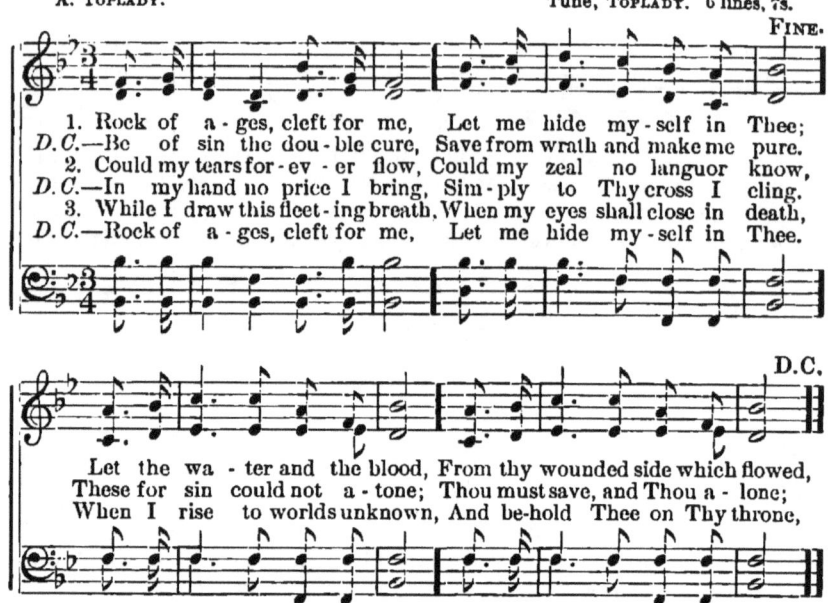

1. Rock of a-ges, cleft for me, Let me hide my-self in Thee;
D.C.—Be of sin the dou-ble cure, Save from wrath and make me pure.
2. Could my tears for-ev-er flow, Could my zeal no languor know,
D.C.—In my hand no price I bring, Sim-ply to Thy cross I cling.
3. While I draw this fleet-ing breath, When my eyes shall close in death,
D.C.—Rock of a-ges, cleft for me, Let me hide my-self in Thee.

Let the wa-ter and the blood, From thy wounded side which flowed,
These for sin could not a-tone; Thou must save, and Thou a-lone;
When I rise to worlds unknown, And be-hold Thee on Thy throne,

No. 25.
1 Quiet, Lord, my wayward heart,
  Make me teachable and mild,
Upright, simple, free from art.
  Make me as a weaned child,
From distrust and envy free,
Pleased with all that pleases Thee.

2 What Thou shalt to-day provide,
  Let me as a child receive;
What to morrow may betide,
  Calmly to Thy wisdom leave;
'Tis enough that Thou wilt care;
Why should I the burden bear?

3 As a little child relies
  On a care beyond his own,
Knows he's neither strong nor wise
  Fears to stir a step alone;
Let me thus with Thee abide,
As my Father, Guard, and Guide.

No. 26.
1 From the cross uplifted high,
  Where the Saviour deigns to die,
What melodious sounds we hear,
Bursting on the ravished ear!
"Love's redeeming work is done;
Come and welcome, sinner, come!"

2 "Sprinkled now with blood the throne;
Why beneath thy burdens groan?
On My pierced body laid,
Justice owns the ransom paid;
Bow the knee, and kiss the Son,
Come and welcome, sinner, come!

3 "Spread for thee, the festal board
See with richest dainties stored;
To thy Father's bosom prest,
Yet again a child confest,
Never from His house to roam,
Come and welcome, sinner, come!

4 "Soon the days of life shall end;
Lo I come, your Saviour, Friend,
Safe your spirit to convey
To the realms of endless day:
Up to My eternal home,
Come and welcome, sinner, come!"

No. 28. The Crowning Day.

"They shall see the Son of man coming in the clouds of heaven, with power and great glory."—Mat. 24: 30.

El. Nathan.   James McGranahan, by per.

1. Our Lord is now re-ject-ed, And by the world disowned
2. The heav'ns shall glow with splendor, But bright-er far than they
3. Our pain shall then be o-ver, We'll sin and sigh no more,
4. Let all that look for, has-ten The com-ing joy-ful day,

By the *ma-ny* still neg-lect-ed, And by the *few* enthroned,
The saints shall shine in glo-ry, As Christ shall them array;
Be-hind us all of sor-row, And nought but joy be-fore,
By ear-nest con-se-cra-tion, To walk the nar-row way.

But soon He'll come in glo-ry, The hour is draw-ing nigh.
The beau-ty of the Sav-ior, Shall daz-zle ev-ery eye·
A joy in our Re-deem-er, As we to Him are nigh,
By gath-'ring in the lost ones, For whom our Lord did die,

For the crown-ing day is com-ing bye and bye.
In the crown-ing day that's com-ing bye and bye.
In the crown-ing day that's com-ing bye and bye.
For the crown-ing day that's com-ing bye and bye.

Copyright, 1881, by Jas. McGranahan.

The Crowning Day.

REFRAIN.

Oh, the crowning day is com-ing Is com-ing bye and bye,
When our Lord shall come in "pow-er," And "glo-ry" from on high
Oh, the glo-rious sight will glad-den Each wait-ing, watch-ful eye,
In the crown-ing day that's com-ing bye and bye.

No. 29.   **Bethany. 6s & 4s.**   **Key G.**

1 Nearer, my God to Thee.
Nearer to Thee!
E'en though it be a cross
That raiseth me;
Still all my songs shall be—
Nearer, my God, to Thee!
Nearer to Thee!

2 Though, like a wanderer,
The sun gone down;
Darkness be over me,
My rest a stone:
Yet in my dreams I'd be—
Nearer, my God, to Thee!
Nearer to Thee!

3 There let the way appear,
Steps unto heaven;
All that Thou sendest me,
In mercy given;
Angels to beckon me—
Nearer, my God, to Thee!
Nearer to Thee.

5 Or if on joyful wing,
Cleaving the sky,
Sun, moon, and stars forgot,
Upward I fly.
Still all my song shall be—
Nearer, my God, to Thee!
Nearer to Thee!

No. 32.

1 Oh for a thousand tongues to sing
　My dear Redeemer's praise!
　The glories of my God and King,
　The triumphs of His grace.

2 My gracious Master and my God,
　Assist me to proclaim,
　To spread through all the earth abroad
　The honors of Thy name.

3 Jesus! the name that calms our fears,
　That bids our sorrows cease—

'Tis music to my ravished ears,
'Tis life, and health, and peace.

4 He breaks the power of reigning sin,
　He sets the prisoner free;
　His blood can make the foulest clean,
　His blood avails for me.

5 Let us obey, we then shall know,
　Shall feel our sins forgiven;
　Anticipate our heaven below,
　And own that love is heaven.

No. 34. Sun of My Soul.

The Lord God is a sun.— Ps. 74:11.

JOHN KEBLE, 1827.   German. Arr. by W. H. MONK.

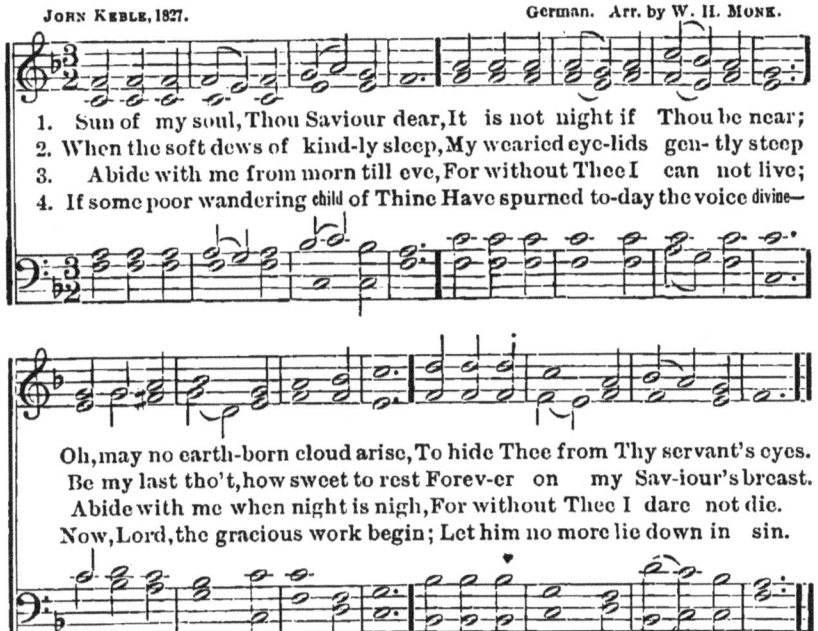

1. Sun of my soul, Thou Saviour dear, It is not night if Thou be near;
2. When the soft dews of kind-ly sleep, My wearied eye-lids gen- tly steep
3. Abide with me from morn till eve, For without Thee I can not live;
4. If some poor wandering child of Thine Have spurned to-day the voice divine—

Oh, may no earth-born cloud arise, To hide Thee from Thy servant's eyes.
Be my last tho't, how sweet to rest Forev-er on my Sav-iour's breast.
Abide with me when night is nigh, For without Thee I dare not die.
Now, Lord, the gracious work begin; Let him no more lie down in sin.

5 Watch by the sick; enrich the poor
With blessings from Thy boundless store;
Be every mourner's sleep to-night,
Like infant's slumbers, pure and light.

6 Come near and bless us when we wake,
Ere thro' the world our way we take,
Till in the ocean of Thy love
We lose ourselves in heaven above.

No. 35.

1 Why will ye waste on trifling cares
That life which God's compassion spares,
While, in the various range of thought,
The one thing needful is forgot?

2 Shall God invite you from above—
Shall Jesus urge his dying love—
Shall troubled conscience give you pain—
And all these pleas unite in vain?

3 Not so your eyes will always view
Those objects which you now pursue;
Not so will heaven and hell appear,
When death's decisive hour is near.

4 Almighty God! thy grace impart;
Fix deep conviction on each heart:
Nor let us waste on trifling cares
That life which thy compassion spares.   P. DODDRIDGE.

No. 36.

1 Jesus, engrave it on my heart,
That thou the one thing needful art;
I could from all things parted be,
But never, never, Lord, from thee.

2 Needful is thy most precious blood,
To reconcile my soul to God;
Needful is thy indulgent care;
Needful thy all-prevailing prayer.

3 Needful art thou, my guide, my stay,
Through all life's dark and weary way;
Nor less in death thou'lt needful be,
To bring my spirit home to thee.

4 Then needful still, my God, my King,
Thy name eternally I'll sing!
Glory and praise be ever his—
The one thing needful Jesus is!   S. MEDLEY.

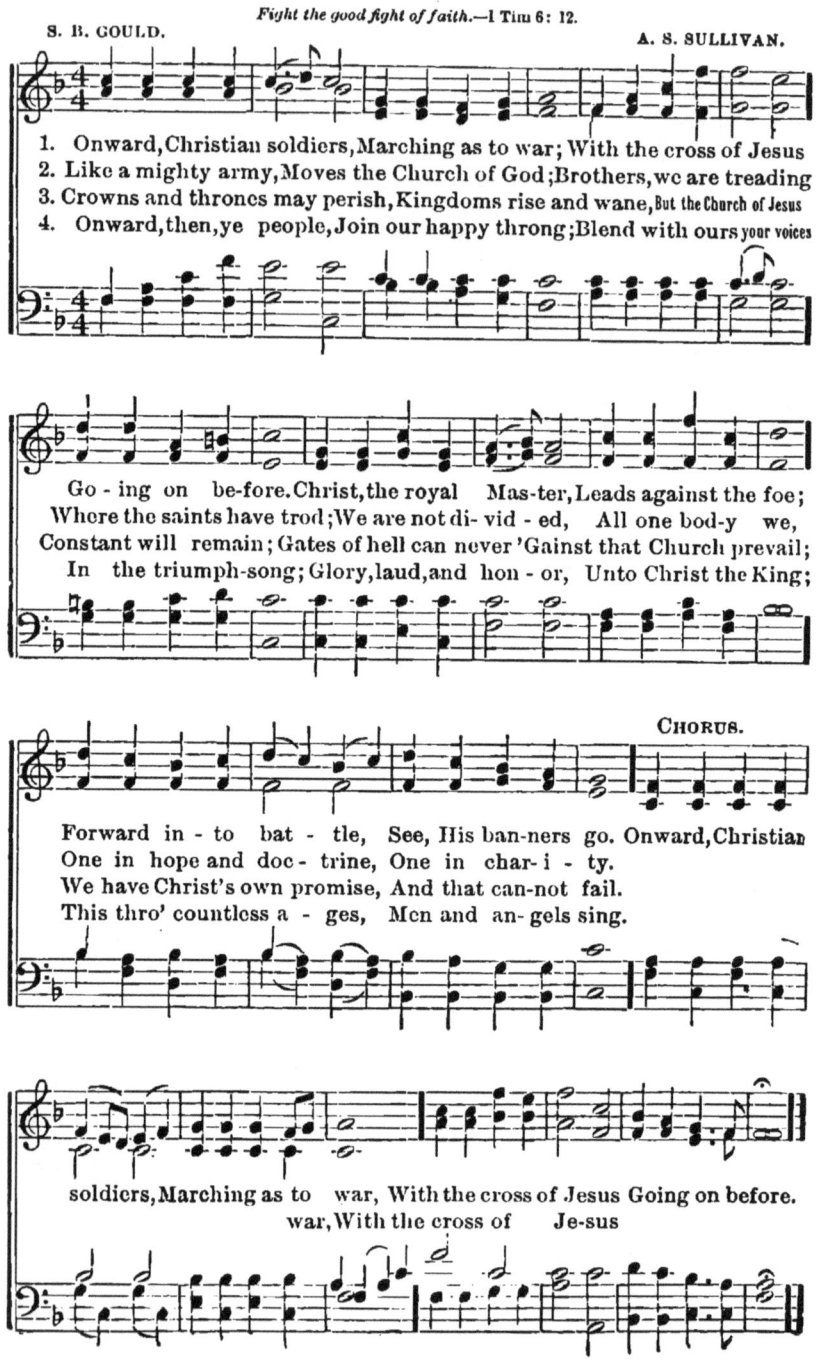

No. 38. I Hear Thy Welcome Voice.

"Come unto Me, all ye that labor and are heavy-laden, and I will give you rest." Matt. 11:28.

Rev. L. HARTSOUGH.   Rev. LEWIS HARTSOUGH, by per

1. I hear Thy welcome voice, That calls me, Lord, to Thee, For
2. Tho' coming weak and vile, Thou dost my strength assure;Thou
3. 'Tis Je-sus calls me on To per-fect faith and love, To
4. 'Tis Je-sus who con-firms The bless-ed work with-in, By
5. And He the wit-ness gives To loy-al hearts and free,That
6. All hail, a-ton-ing blood! All hail, re-deem-ing grace! All

CHORUS.

cleansing in Thy precious blood, That flow'd on Calvary. I am coming,
dost my vileness ful-ly cleanse, Till spot-less all and pure.
per-fect hope, and peace and trust. For earth and heav'n above.
add-ing grace to welcom'd grace, Where reigned the pow'r of sin.
ev-'ry promise is ful-filled, If faith but brings the plea.
hail, the Gift of Christ, our Lord, Our strength, and Righteousness!

Lord,coming now to Thee, Wash me, cleanse me in the blood, That flowed on Calvary.

By per. Phillip Phillips, Copyright in "Song Sermons."

No. 39.
E. P. PRENTISS

1 More love to Thee, O Christ!
   More love to Thee!
  Hear, Thou, the prayer I make
   On bended knee;
  This is my earnest plea,—
  More love, O Christ, to Thee,
   More love to Thee!

2 Once earthly joy I craved,
   Sought peace and rest;
  Now Thee alone I seek,
   Give what is best:
  This all my prayer shall be,—
  More love, O Christ, to Thee,
   More love to Thee!

3 Let sorrow do its work,
   Send grief and pain;
  Sweet are Thy messengers,
   Sweet their refrain,
  When they can sing with me,—
  More love, O Christ, to Thee,
   More love to Thee!

4 Then shall my latest breath
   Whisper Thy praise;
  This be the parting cry
   My heart shall raise —
  This still its prayer shall be,—
  More love, O Christ, to Thee,
   More love to Thee.

Lenox 6s & 8s. LEWIS EDSON, 1782.

No. 43.

1 Oh. for a shout of joy,
  Worthy the theme we sing;
  To this divine employ
  Our hearts and voices bring;
  Sound, sound, thro' all the earth abroad,
  The love, the eternal love of God.

2 Unnumbered myriads stand,
  Of seraphs bright and fair,
  Or bow at thy right hand,
  And pay their homage there;
  But strive in vain with loudest chord,
  To sound thy wondrous love, O Lord.

3 Yet sinners saved by grace,
  In songs of lower key,
  In every age and place,
  Have sung the mystery,—
  Have told in strains of sweet accord,
  Thy love, thy sovereign love, O Lord.

No. 44.

1 Come, every pious heart,
  That loves the Saviour's name,
  Your noblest powers exert
  To celebrate his fame;
  Tell all above, and all below,
  The debt of love to him you owe.

2 He left His starry crown,
  And laid His robes aside.
  On wings of love came down,
  And wept, and bled, and died;
  What he endured, oh, who can tell,
  To save our souls from death and hell?

3 From the dark grave he rose,
  The mansion of the dead,
  And thence his mighty foes
  In glorious triumph led;   [rode,
  Up through the sky the Conqueror
  And reigns on high, the Saviour, God.
  S. STENNETT.

No. 45.

1 Lord of the worlds above,
  How pleasant and how fair
  The dwellings of Thy love,
  Thine earthly temples are!
  To thine abode
    My heart aspires,
    With warm desires
  To see my God.

2 O happy souls, that pray
  Where God appoints to hear.
  O happy men, that pay
  Their constant service there!
  They praise Thee still;
    And happy they
    That love the way
  To Zion's hill.

3 They go from strength, to strength,
  Through this dark vale of tears,
  Till each arrives at length,
  Till each in heaven appears.
  O glorious seat,
    When God our King
    Shall thither bring
  Our willing feet!

No. 47. My Jesus, I Love Thee.

"Mine are thine and thine are mine."—John 17: 10.

London Hymn Book, 1864. A. J. GORDON. By per.

1. My Jesus, I love Thee, I know Thou art mine,
   For Thee all the follies of sin I resign;
   My gracious Redeemer, my Saviour art Thou,
   If ever I loved Thee, my Jesus, 'tis now.

2. I love Thee, because Thou hast first loved me,
   And purchased my pardon on Calvary's tree;
   I love Thee for wearing the thorns on Thy brow;
   If ever I loved Thee, my Jesus, 'tis now.

3. I will love Thee in life, I will love Thee in death,
   And praise Thee as long as Thou lendest me breath;
   And say when the death-dew lies cold on my brow,
   If ever I loved Thee, my Jesus, 'tis now.

4. In mansions of glory and endless delight,
   I'll ever adore Thee in heaven so bright;
   I'll sing with the glittering crown on my brow,
   If ever I loved Thee, my Jesus, 'tis now.

No. 48. Blest be the Tie.

Rev. John Fawcett, 1772. From H. G. Nageli.

1. Blest be the tie that binds Our hearts in Christian love;
2. Before our Father's throne, We pour our ardent prayers;
3. We share our mutual woes; Our mutual burdens bear;
4. When we asunder part, It gives us inward pain:

The fellowship of kindred minds Is like to that above.
Our fears, our hopes, our aims are one,— Our comforts and our cares.
And ofter for each other flows The sympathizing tear.
But we shall still be joined in heart, And hope to meet again.

No. 49.

1 Oh, where shall rest be found—
  Rest for the weary soul? [sound,
  'Twere vain the ocean depths to
  Or pierce to either pole.

2 The world can never give
  The bliss for which we sigh:
  'Tis not the whole of life to live,
  Nor all of death to die.

3 Beyond this vale of tears
  There is a life above,
  Unmeasured by the flight of years;
  And all that life is love.

4 There is a death whose pang
  Outlasts the fleeting breath;
  Oh, what eternal horrors hang
  Around the second death!

5 Lord God of truth and grace!
  Teach us that death to shun;
  Lest we be banished from thy face,
  And evermore undone.

J. Montgomery.

No. 50.

1 How gentle God's commands!
  How kind his precepts are!
  Come, cast your burdens on the Lord,
  And trust his constant care.

2 Beneath his watchful eye
  His saints securely dwell;
  That hand which bears creation up
  Shall guard his children well.

3 Why should this anxious load
  Press down your weary mind?
  Haste to your heavenly Father's throne,
  And sweet refreshment find.

4 His goodness stand approved,
  Unchanged from day to day:
  I'll drop my burden at his feet,
  And bear a song away.

P. Doddridge.

No. 51. Seeking for Me.

"For the Son of Man is come to seek and save that which was lost."—Luke 19: 10.

E. E. Hasty. By per.

1. Je-sus, my Saviour, to Beth-lehem came, Born in a man-ger to
2. Je-sus, my Saviour, on Cal-vary's tree, Paid the great debt, and my
3. Je-sus, my Saviour, the same as of old, While I did wan-der a-
4. Je-sus, my Saviour, shall come from on high, Sweet is the promise as

sorrow and shame; Oh! it was wonderful! blest be His name! Seeking for me, for
soul He set free; Oh! it was wonderful! how could it be? Dying for me, for
far from the fold, Gently and long He hath plead with my soul, Calling for me, for
weary years fly; Oh! I shall see Him descending the sky, Coming for me, for

for me, . . . for me, ...

me, Seeking for me, Seeking for me, Seeking for me, Seeking for me,
me, Dying for me, Dying for me, Dying for me, Dying for me,
me, Calling for me, Calling for me, Calling for me, Calling for me,
me, Coming for me, Coming for me, Coming for me, Coming for me,

Oh, it was wonderful! blest be His name! Seeking for me, for me.
Oh, it was wonderful! how could it be? Dying for me, for me.
Gently and long He hath plead with my soul, Calling for me, for me.
Oh, I shall see Him descending the sky, Coming for me, for me.

No. 52.   Scotland. 12s.   J. Clark.

1. The voice of free grace cries es-cape to the mountain,
For A-dam's lost race Christ hath o-pened a fountain;
For sin and un-clean-ness, and ev-'ry trans-gres-sion,
Hal-le-lu-jah to the Lamb, who hath purchased our par-don,
His blood flows most freely in streams of sal-va-tion,
We'll praise Him a-gain, when we pass o-ver Jor-dan.
His blood flows most free-ly in streams of sal-va-tion.
We'll praise Him a-gain, when we pass o-ver Jor-dan.

2 Ye souls that are wounded, O flee to the Saviour! [favor;
He calls you in mercy, 'tis infinite
Your sins are increasing, escape to the mountain,—
His blood can remove them; it flows from the fountain.
Hallelujah to the Lamb, etc.

3 With joy shall we stand when es-caped to the shore;
With harps in our hands we will praise Him the more!
We'll range the sweet plains on the banks of the river, [ever
And sing of salvation for ever and
Hallelujah to the Lamb, etc.

No. 54. Holy, Holy! Lord God Almighty!

"They rest not day nor night, saying, Holy, Holy, Holy, Lord God Almighty, which was, and is, and is to come."—Rev. 4: 8.

REGINALD HEBER, D. D.   Rev. JOHN B. DYKES.

1. Ho ly, Ho ly, Ho - ly! Lord God Al-migh - ty!
2. Ho ly, Ho ly, Ho ly! all the saints a - dore Thee,
3. Ho - ly, Ho ly, Ho - ly! tho' the darkness hide Thee,
4. Ho - ly, Ho - ly, Ho - ly! Lord God Al-migh - ty!

Ear - ly in the morn - ing our song shall rise to Thee;
Cast-ing down their golden crowns a - round the glass - y sea;
Though the eye of sin - ful man Thy glo - ry may not see,
All Thy works shall praise Thy name in earth, and sky, and sea;

Ho - ly, Ho - ly, Ho - ly! Mer-ci - ful and Migh - ty!
Cher - u - bim and Ser - aphim fall-ing down be - fore Thee,
On - ly Thou art Ho - ly, there is none be - side Thee,
Ho ly, Ho - ly, Ho - ly! Mer-ci - ful and Migh - ty!

God in three Per - sons, bless-ed Trin - i - ty!
Which wert and art, and ev - er-more shalt be.
Per - fect in pow'r, in love, and pu - ri - ty.
God in three Per - sons, bless-ed Trin - i - ty! A - men.

No. 56. Antioch.

WATTS.   HANDEL.

1. Joy to the world, the Lord is come! Let earth re-ceive her King; Let ev-'ry heart prepare Him room, And heav'n and na-ture sing, And heav'n and na-ture sing, And heav'n, and heav'n and na-ture sing.

2 Joy to the world, the Saviour reigns,
   Let men their songs employ;
While fields and floods, rocks, hills
   and plains
Repeat the sounding joy.

3 No more let sin and sorrow grow,
   Nor thorns infest the ground;
He comes to make His blessings flow
   Far as the curse is found.

4 He rules the world with truth and
   grace,
And make the nations prove
The glories of His righteousness
And wonders of His love.

No. 57.

1 Come, we that love the Lord,
   And let our joys be known,
Join in a song with sweet accord,
Join in a song with sweet accord,
And thus surround the throne,
And thus surround the throne.

CHO.—We're marching to Zion,
   Beautiful, beautiful Zion;
We're marching upward to Zion,
   The beautiful city of God.

2 Let those refuse to sing
   Who never knew our God;
But children of the heav'nly King,
But children of the heav'nly King,
May speak their joys abroad,
May speak their joys abroad.

3 The hill of Zion yields
   A thousand sacred sweets,
Before we reach the heav'nly fields,
Before we reach the heav'nly fields,
Or walk the golden streets,
Or walk the golden streets.

4 Then let our songs abound,
   And every tear be dry;
We're marching thro' Immanuel's
   ground,
We're marching thro' Immanuel's
   ground,
To fairer worlds on high,
To fairer worlds on high.

No. 58. Deliverance will Come.

We are journeying unto the place of which the Lord said, I will give it you.—Num. 10: 29.

J. B. M. REV. J. B. MATTHIAS, 1836.

1. I saw a wayworn trav'ler In tatter'd garments clad,
His back was laden heavy, His strength was almost gone,
And struggling up the mountain, It seemed that he was sad;
Yet he shouted as he journeyed, Deliverance will come.

2. The summer sun was shining, The sweat was on his brow,
But he kept pressing onward, For he was wending home;
His garments worn and dusty, His step seemed very slow:
Still shouting as he journeyed, Deliverance will come.

3. The songsters in the arbor, That stood beside the way,
His watchword being "Onward!" He stopped his ears and ran,
Attracted his attention, Inviting his delay:
Still shouting as he journeyed, Deliverance will come.

CHORUS.

Then palms of victory, crowns of glory, Palms of victory I shall wear.

4 I saw him in the evening,
The sun was bending low;
He'd overtopped the mountain,
And reached the vale below:
He saw the golden city,—
His everlasting home,—
And shouted loud, Hosanna,
Deliverance will come!

5 While gazing on that city,
Just o'er the narrow flood,
A band of holy angels
Came from the throne of God:

They bore him on their pinions
Safe o'er the dashing foam,
And joined him in his triumph—
Deliverance has come!

6 I heard the song of triumph
They sang upon that shore,
Saying, Jesus has redeemed us
To suffer nevermore:
Then, casting his eyes backward
On the race which he had run,
He shouted loud, Hosanna,
Deliverance has come!

5 Ho! all ye heavy-laden, come?
  Here's pardon, comfort, rest and home;
  Ye wanderers from a Father's face,
  Return, accept His proffered grace.
  Ye tempted ones, there's refuge nigh,
  "Jesus of Nazareth passeth by."

6 But if you still this call refuse,
  And all His wondrous love abuse,
  Soon will He sadly from you turn,
  Your bitter prayer for pardon spurn.
  "Too late! too late!" will be the cry—
  "Jesus of Nazareth *has passed by.*"

No. 62.   Italian Hymn.

Words by C. Wesley. F. Ciardini, 1769.

1. Come, Thou Al-might-y King, Help us Thy name to sing;
2. Come, Thou In-car-nate Word, Gird on Thy might-y sword,
3. Come, Ho-ly Com-fort-er, Thy sa-cred wit-ness bear,
4. To the great One in Three, The high-est prais-es be,

Help us to praise! Fa-ther all glo-ri-ous, O'er all vic-
Our pray'r at-tend; Come and Thy peo-ple bless, And give thy
In this glad hour; Thou who al-might-y art, Now rule in
Hence ev-er-more! His sov'reign ma-jes-ty, May we in

to-ri-ous, Come and reign o-ver us, An-cient of Days.
word suc-cess; Spir-it of ho-li-ness, On us de-scend.
ev-'ry heart, And ne'er from us de-part, Spir-it of power.
glo-ry see, And to e-ter-ni-ty, Love and a-dore.

No. 63.

1 Come, Holy Ghost! in love,
  Shed on us, from above.
  Thine own bright ray:
  Divinely good Thou art;
  Thy sacred gifts impart,
  To gladden each sad heart;
  Oh! come to-day!

2 Come, tenderest Friend, and best,
  Our most delightful Guest!
  With soothing power;
  Rest, which the weary know;
  Shade, 'mid the noontide glow;
  Peace, when deep griefs o'erflow;
  Cheer us, this hour!

3 Come, Light serene! and still
  Our inmost bosoms fill;
  Dwell in each breast;
  We know no dawn but thine;
  Send forth Thy beams divine,
  On our dark souls to shine,
  And make us blest.

4 Exalt our low desires;
  Extinguish passions fires;
  Heal every wound;
  Our stubborn spirits bend;
  Our icy coldness end;
  Our devious steps attend,
  While heavenward bound.

Rathbun. 8s & 7s.   ITHAMAR CONKEY.

No. 67.

1 Holy Ghost, dispel our sadness,
  Pierce the clouds of sinful night;
 Come, Thou Source of sweetest gladness,
  Breathe Thy life and spread Thy [light.

2 From that height which knows no measure,
  As a gracious shower, descend,
 Bringing down the richest treasure
  Man can wish, or God can send!

3 Come, Thou best of all donations
  God can give, or we implore;
 Having Thy sweet consolations,
  We need wish for nothing more.

4 Author of the new creation,
  Let us now Thy influence prove;
 Make our hearts Thy habitation,
  Shed abroad a Saviour's love.

5 Hear, oh hear our supplication,
  Blessed Jesus, God of peace,
 Rest upon this congregation,
  With the fullness of Thy grace.

No. 68.

1 Hail! my ever blessed Jesus,
   Only thee I wish to sing;
  To my soul Thy name is precious,
   Thou my Prophet, Priest and King.
  O! what mercy flows from heaven!
   O! what joy and happiness!
  Love I much? I'm much forgiven,
   I'm a miracle of grace.

2 Once with Adam's race in ruin,
   Unconcerned in sin I lay;
  Swift destruction still pursuing,
   Till my Saviour passed that way.
  Witness, all ye hosts of heaven,
   My Redeemer's tenderness;
  Love I much? I'm much forgiven,
   I'm a miracle of grace.

3 Shout, ye bright angelic choir,
   Praise the Lamb enthroned above;
  While astonished I admire [love.
   God's free grace and boundless
  That blest moment I received Him,
   Filled my soul with joy and peace;
  Love I much? I'm much forgiven,
   I'm a miracle of grace.

No. 69.

1 Look, ye saints! the sight is glorious
   See the man of sorrows now,
  From the fight returned victorious;—
   Every knee to Him shall bow:
  ‖:Crown Him—crown Him!—
   Crowns become the victor's brow.:‖

2 Crown the Saviour, angels! crown Him:
   Rich the trophies Jesus brings:
  In the seat of power enthrone Him,
   While the vault of heaven rings:
  ‖: Crown Him—crown Him!—
   Crown the Saviour, King of kings.:‖

3 Hark! those bursts of acclamation!
   Hark! those loud triumphant chords!
  Jesus takes the highest station;—
   O what joy the sight affords!
  ‖: Crown Him—crown Him,—
   King of kings, and Lord of lords!:‖

No. 70.

1 Saviour, visit Thy plantation,
   Grant us, Lord, a gracious rain;
  All will come to desolation,
   Unless Thou return again.

2 Keep no longer at a distance,
   Shine upon us from on high,
  Lest, for want of Thine assistance,
   Every plant should droop and die.

3 Let our mutual love be fervent;
   Make us prevalent in prayer;
  Let each one esteemed Thy servant
   Shun the world's bewitching snare.

4 Break the tempter's fatal power,
   Turn the stony heart to flesh,
  And begin from this good hour
   To revive Thy work afresh.

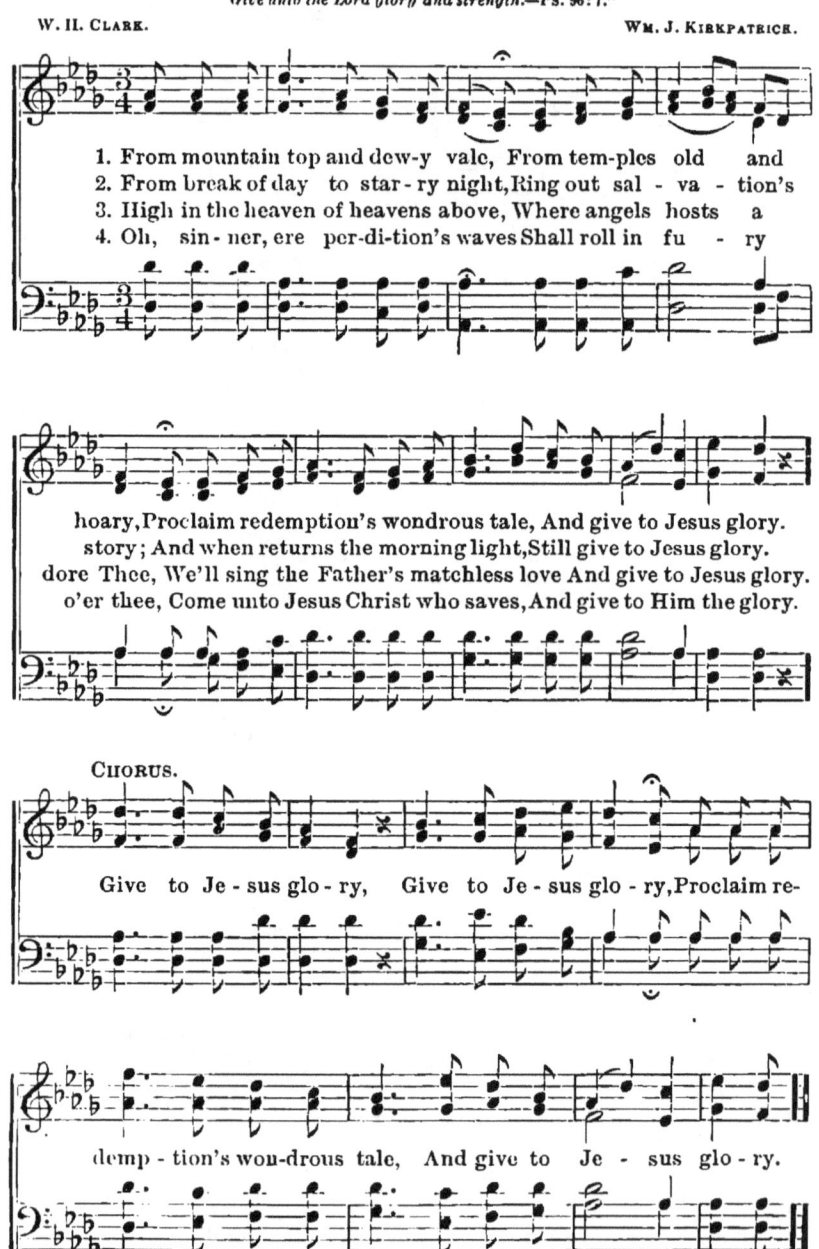

Arlington. C. M.   Dr. Arne.

No. 72.

1 Am I a soldier of the cross,—
  A follower of the Lamb,—
  And shall I fear to own his cause,
  Or blush to speak his name?

2 Are there no foes for me to face?
  Must I not stem the flood?
  Is this vile world a friend to grace,
  To help me on to God?

3 Sure I must fight if I would reign;
  Increase my courage, Lord!
  I'll bear the toil, endure the pain,
  Supported by thy word.

No. 73.

1 Come, Holy Spirit, heavenly Dove,
  With all thy quickening powers·
  Kindle a flame of sacred love
  In these cold hearts of ours.

2 Father, and shall we ever live
  At this poor dying rate,
  Our love so faint, so cold to thee,
  And thine to us so great?

3 Come, Holy Spirit, heavenly Dove,
  With all thy quickening powers;
  Come, shed abroad a Savior's love,
  And that shall kindle ours.

Nettleton. 8. 7. 4.

No. 74.

1 Come thou Fount of every blessing,
  Tune my heart to sing thy grace;
  Streams of mercy, never ceasing,
  Call for songs of loudest praise.
  Teach me some melodious sonnet,
  Sung by flaming tongues above;
  Praise the mount— I'm fixed upon it—
  Mount of thy redeeming love.

2 Here I'll raise mine Ebenezer;
  Hither by thy help I'm come;
  And I hope by thy good pleasure,
  Safely to arrive at home.
  Jesus sought me when a stranger;
  Wandering from the fold of God
  He, to rescue me from danger,
  Interposed his precious blood.

3 O to grace how great a debtor
  Daily I'm constrained to be!
  Let thy goodness like a fetter,
  Bind my wandering heart to thee:
  Prone to wander, Lord, I feel it,
  Prone to leave the God I love;
  Here's my heart, O take and seal it;
  Seal it for thy courts above.

No. 75.
                    Key F.

1 What a friend we have in Jesus.
  All our sins and griefs to bear;
  What a privilege to carry
  Everything to God in prayer?
  Oh, what peace we often forfeit,
  Oh, what needless pain we bear—
  All because we do not carry
  Everything to God in prayer.

2 Have we trials and temptations?
  Is there trouble anywhere?
  We should never be discouraged,
  Take it to the Lord in prayer.
  Can we find a Friend so faithful,
  Who will all our sorrows share?
  Jesus knows our every weakness,
  Take it to the Lord in prayer.

3 Are we weak and heavy laden,
  Cumbered with a load of care?
  Precious Savior, still our refuge,
  Take it to the Lord in prayer.
  Do thy friends despise, forsake thee?
  Take it to the Lord in prayer;
  In His arms he'll take and shield thee,
  Thou wilt find a solace there.

No. 76. Come to Jesus, just now.

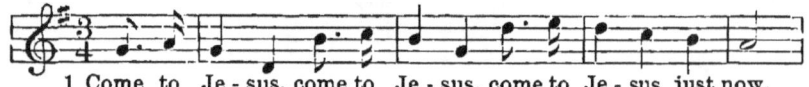
1 Come to Je-sus, come to Je-sus, come to Je-sus just now,

Just now come to Je-sus, come to Je-sus just now.

2 He will save you.	6 O believe Him.	10 He will cleanse you.
3 He is able.	7 O receive Him.	11 Only trust Him.
4 He is willing.	8 Jesus loves you.	12 Let us praise Him.
5 He is waiting.	9 He will bless you.	13 Hallelujah. Amen.

No. 77. Angels Hovering Round.

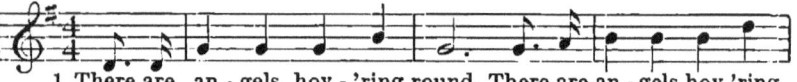
1 There are an-gels hov-'ring round, There are an-gels hov-'ring

round, There are an - gels, an - gels hov-'ring round.

2 To carry the tidings home, etc.
3 To the New Jerusalem, etc.
4 Poor sinners are coming home, etc.
5 And Jesus bids them come, etc.
6 There's glory all around, etc.

78. Sweet By and By.   79. Over There.

 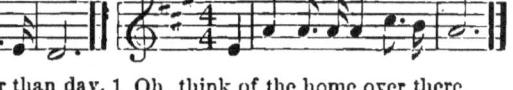

1 There's a land that is fairer than day.
And by faith we can see it afar
For the Father waits over the way
To prepare us a dwelling place there.

CHORUS.

In the sweet by and by
We shall meet on that beautiful shore,
In the sweet by and by
We shall meet on that beautiful shore.

2 We shall sing on that beautiful shore,
The melodious songs of the blest,
And our spirits shall sorrow no more
Not a sigh for the blessing of rest.

3 To our bountiful Father above
We will offer the tribute of praise
For the glorious gift of His love
And the blessings that hallow our days.

By per. O. Ditson & Co.

1 Oh, think of the home over there,
By the side of the river of light,
Where the saints all immortal and fair
Are robed in their garments of white.

CHORUS.

Over there, over there,
Oh, think of the home over there,
Over there, over there,
Oh, think of the home over there.

2 Oh, think of the friends over there,
Who before us the journey have trod,
Of the songs that they breathe on the air
In their home in the palace of God.

3 I'll soon be at home over there,
For the end of my journey I see.
Many dear to my heart over there
Are watching and waiting for me

Ortonville: C: M:

No. 80.
1 Majestic sweetness sits enthroned
    Upon the Savior's brow;
His head with radiant glories crowned,
    His lips with grace o'erflow.

2 No mortal can with Him compare,
    Among the sons of men;
Fairer is He than all the fair
    Who fill the heavenly train.

3 He saw me plunged in deep distress,
    And flew to my relief,
For me He bore the shameful cross,
    And carried all my grief.

No. 81.
1 My hope is built on nothing less,
    Than Jesus' blood and righteousness,
I dare not trust the sweetest frame,
    But wholly lean on Jesus' name.
    On Christ the solid Rock I stand:
    All other ground is sinking sand,
    All other ground is sinking sand.

2 When darkness veils His lovely face,
    I rest on His unchanging grace;
In every high and stormy gale,
    My anchor holds within the vail.

3 His oath, His covenant, His blood,
    Support me in the whelming flood;
When all around my soul gives way,
    He then is all my hope and stay.

4 When He shall come with trumpet sound,
    O, may I then in Him be found;
Drest in His righteousness alone,
    Faultless to stand before the throne!

No. 82.
1 Sweet hour of prayer, sweet hour of prayer!
That calls me from a world of care
And bids me at my Father's throne
Make all my wants and wishes known;
In seasons of distress and grief,
My soul has often found relief;
:|:And oft escaped the tempter's snare,
By thy return, sweet hour of prayer. :|:

2 Sweet hour of prayer, sweet hour of prayer!
Thy wings shall my petition bear
To Him, whose truth and faithfulness
Engage the waiting soul to bless.
And since He bids me seek His face,
Believe his word, and trust His grace,
:|:I'll cast on Him my every care,
And wait for thee, sweet hour of pray-

No. 83. [er!:|:
1 Amazing grace! how sweet the sound
    That saved a wretch like me!
I once was lost, but now am found,
    Was blind, but now I see.

2 'Twas grace that taught my heart to
    And grace my fears relieved; [fear.
How precious did that grace appear,
    The hour I first believed.

4 Thro' many dangers, toils and snares,
    I have already come;
'Tis grace that brought me safe thus far,
    And grace will lead me home.

No. 84.
1 Lord, I hear of showers of blessing
    Thou art scattering full and free—
Showers the thirsty land refreshing;
    Let some droppings fall on me—
    Even me, even me,
    Let Thy blessing fall on me.

2 Pass me not, O gracious Father!
    Sinful though my heart may be;
Thou might'st leave me, but the rather
    Let Thy mercy fall on me.

3 Pass me not, O tender Savior!
    Let me love and cling to Thee:
I am longing for Thy favor;
    Whilst Thou'rt calling, oh, call me.

4 Pass me not, O mighty Spirit!
    Thou can'st make the blind to see;
Witnesser of Jesus' merit,
    Speak the word of power to me.

5 Love of God, so pure and changeless:
    Blood of Christ, so rich and free;
Grace of God, so strong and boundless,
    Magnify them all in me.

6 Pass me not! Thy lost one bringing,
    Bind my heart, O Lord, to Thee;
While the streams of life are springing,
    Blessing others, oh, bless me.

No. 86.   **Hendon.**   **7s.**   Rev. Dr. Malan.

1. Lord, we come before Thee now,— At Thy feet we humbly bow, Oh, do not our suit disdain! Shall we seek Thee, Lord, in vain?
2. Lord, on Thee our souls depend; In compassion, now descend; Fill our hearts with Thy rich grace, Tune our lips to sing Thy praise.
3. In Thy own appointed way, Now we seek Thee, here we stay; Lord, we know not how to go, Till a blessing Thou bestow.
4. Send some message from Thy word, That may peace and joy afford; Let Thy Spirit now impart Full salvation to each heart.

No. 87.

1 Holy Ghost, with light divine,
Shine upon this heart of mine:
Chase the shades of night away,
Turn my darkness into day.

2 Holy Ghost, with power divine,
Cleanse this guilty heart of mine;
Long hath sin, without control,
Held dominion o'er my soul.

3 Holy Ghost, with joy divine,
Cheer this saddened heart of mine;
Bid my many woes depart,
Heal my wounded, bleeding heart.

1 Holy Spirit, All-Divine,
Dwell within this heart of mine;
Cast down every idol throne,
Reign supreme, and reign alone.

No. 88.

1 Come, my soul, thy suit prepare.
Jesus loves to answer prayer;
He himself has bid thee pray,
Therefore will not say thee nay.

2 With my burden I begin—
Lord! remove this load of sin;
Let thy blood, for sinners spilt,
Set my conscience free from guilt.

3 Lord! I come to the for rest;
Take possession of my breast:
There, thy blood-bought right maintain,
And, without a rival, reign.

4 While I am a pilgrim here,
Let thy love my spirit cheer;
As my Guide, my Guard, my Friend,
Lead me to my journey's end.

5 Show me what I have to do,
Every hour my strength renew;
Let me live a life of faith,
Let me die thy people's death.

J. Newton.

No. 89. Ariel. C. P. M.

Ps. 63d.

Dr. L. Mason.

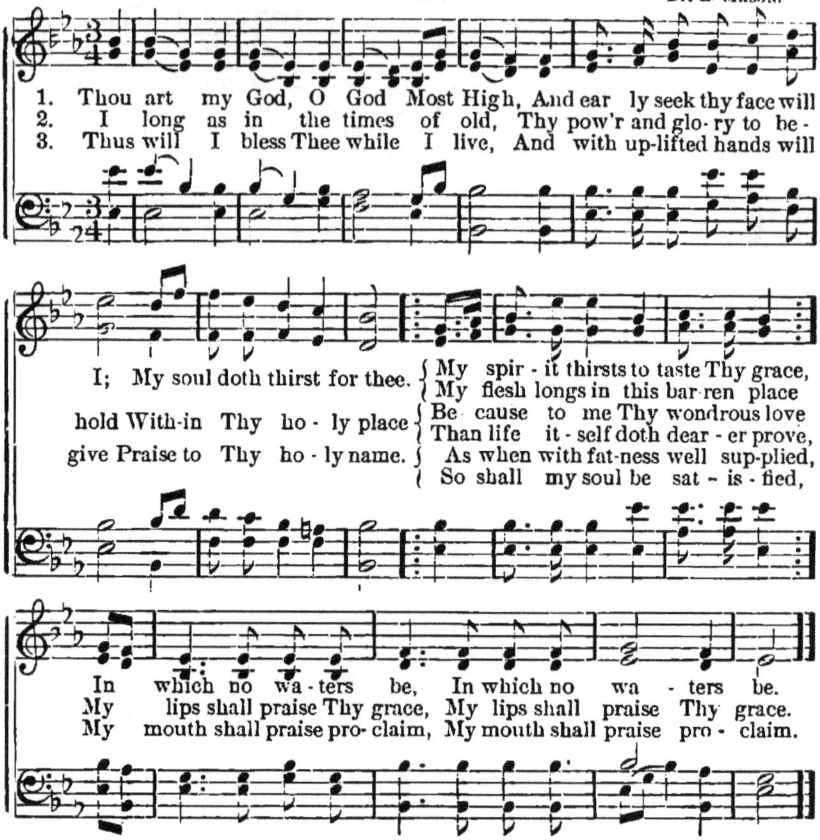

1. Thou art my God, O God Most High, And early seek thy face will
2. I long as in the times of old, Thy pow'r and glory to behold With-in Thy holy place
3. Thus will I bless Thee while I live, And with up-lifted hands will give Praise to Thy holy name.

I; My soul doth thirst for thee.
{ My spirit thirsts to taste Thy grace,
  My flesh longs in this barren place
{ Be cause to me Thy wondrous love
  Than life it-self doth dear-er prove,
{ As when with fat-ness well sup-plied,
  So shall my soul be sat-is-fied,

In which no wa-ters be, In which no wa-ters be.
My lips shall praise Thy grace, My lips shall praise Thy grace.
My mouth shall praise pro-claim, My mouth shall praise pro-claim.

No. 90.

1 O love divine, how sweet thou art!
When shall I find my willing heart
All taken up by thee?
I thirst, I faint, I die to prove
The greatness of redeeming love,—
The love of Christ to me.

2 Stronger his love than death or hell:
No mortal can its riches tell,
Nor first-born sons of light:
In vain they long its depths to see;
They cannot reach the mystery,—
The length, the breadth, the height.

3 God only knows the love of God;
O that it now were shed abroad
In this poor, stony heart!
For love I sigh, for love I pine;
This only portion, Lord, be mine—
Be mine this better part.

4 O that I could forever sit
In transport at my Saviour's feet!
Be this my happy choice;
My only care, delight, and bliss,

My joy, my heaven on earth be this,
To hear my Saviour's voice.

No. 91.

1 Oh, could I speak the matchless worth,
Oh, could I sound the glories forth,
Which in my Saviour shine! [strings
I'd soar, and touch the heavenly
And vie with Gabriel while he sings
In notes almost divine.

2 I'd sing the precious blood he spilt,
My ransom from the dreadful guilt,
Of sin and wrath divine!
I'd sing his glorious righteousness,
In which all-perfect heavenly dress
My soul shall ever shine.

3 Well—the delightful day will come,
When my dear Lord will bring me
And I shall see his face: [home,
Then with my Saviour, Brother,
A blest eternity I'll spend, [Friend,
Triumphant in his grace.

S. Medley.

Take me as I am.

Rev. J. H. Stockton.

Lord, to Thee I cry, Unless Thou help me, I must die;
am, and full of guilt, But yet for me Thy blood was spilt,
work for me to do, Inspire my will, my heart renew,
last the work is done, The bat-tle o'er, the vic-t'ry won,

free sal-va-tion nigh, And take me as I am!
st make me what Thou wilt, But take me as I am!
in and by me too, But take me as I am!
cry shall be a-lone, Oh, take me as I am!

free sal-va-tion nigh, And take me as I am.

I am,...... Take me as I am,...... Oh,
me as I am, Take me, take me as I am;

Copyright, 1878, by John J. Hood.

to be perfectly light;
Poor sinner, harden not thy heart,
live in my soul; Thou would'st be saved—Why not
cast out every to-night?
  [than snow. Cho. :Why not to-night? Why not to-
shall be whiter night? [not to-night?:|
ow, etc, Thou would'st be saved—Why

lown from Thy 2 To-morrow's sun may never rise,
  [sacrifice; To bless thy long deluded sight
ake a complete This is the time! Oh, then be wise!
nd whatever I Thou would'st be saved—Why not
  [than snow. to-night?
shall be whiter 3 The world has nothing left to give—
est I patiently It has no new, no pure delight;
  [create; Oh, try the life which Christians live!
n me a new heart Thou would'st be saved—Why not
e sought Thee, to-night?
No. [than snow. 4 Our blessed Lord refuses none
shall be whiter Who would to him their souls unite;
Then be the work of grace begun!
ord depart, Thou would'st be saved—*Why not*
yes against the *to-night?*

No. 95. Cross and Crown.

"And he bearing his cross, went forth."—John 19: 17.

Tho's Shepherd. Geo. N. Allen.

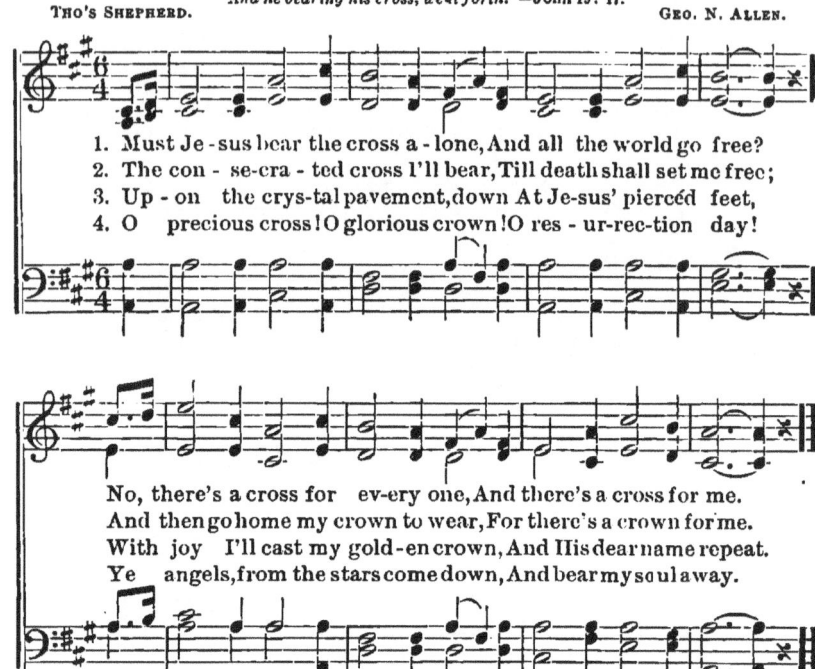

1. Must Jesus bear the cross alone, And all the world go free?
2. The consecrated cross I'll bear, Till death shall set me free;
3. Upon the crystal pavement, down At Jesus' piercéd feet,
4. O precious cross! O glorious crown! O resurrection day!

No, there's a cross for every one, And there's a cross for me.
And then go home my crown to wear, For there's a crown for me.
With joy I'll cast my golden crown, And His dear name repeat.
Ye angels, from the stars come down, And bear my soul away.

No. 96.

1 I've reach'd the land of corn and wine
And all its riches freely mine; [day;
Here shines, undimm'd, one blissful
For all my night has passed away.

CHORUS.

O Beulah Land! sweet Beulah Land!
As on thy highest mount I stand,
I look away across the sea,
Where mansions are prepared for me,
And view the shining glory shore,
My heaven, my home for evermore.

2 My Saviour comes and walks with me,
And sweet communion here have we;
He gently leads me by His hand,
For this is heaven's borderland

3 A sweet perfume upon the breeze
Is borne from ever vernal trees;
And flowers that, never fading, grow
Where streams of life for ever flow.

4 The zephyrs seem to float to me
Sweet sounds of heaven's melody,
As angels, with the white-rob'd throng
Join in the sweet redemption song.

No. 97.

1 The great Physician now is here,
The sympathizing Jesus; [cheer,
He speaks, the drooping heart to
Oh, hear the voice of Jesus.

CHORUS.

Sweetest note in seraph song,
Sweetest name on mortal tongue,
Sweetest carol ever sung,
Jesus, blessed Jesus!

2 Your many sins are all forgiven,
Oh, hear the voice of Jesus.
Go on your way in peace to heaven,
And wear a crown with Jesus.

3 All glory to the dying Lamb!
I now believe in Jesus;
I love the blessed Saviour's name,
I love the name of Jesus.

4 His name dispels my guilt and fear
No other name but Jesus;
Oh, how my soul delights to hear
The precious name of Jesus.

Webb. 7 & 6.

No. 98.

1 In heavenly love abiding,
　No change my heart shall fear,
And safe is such confiding,
　For nothing changes here:
The storm may roar without me,
　My heart may low be laid,
But God is round about me,
　And can I be dismayed?

2 Wherever he may guide me,
　No want shall turn me back;
My Shepherd is beside me,
　And nothing can I lack:
His wisdom ever waketh,
　His sight is never dim:
He knows the way he taketh,
　And I will walk with him.

3 Green pastures are before me,
　Which yet I have not seen;
Bright skies will soon be o'er me,
　Where darkest clouds have been:
My hope I cannot measure;
　My path to life is free;
My Saviour has my treasure,
　And he will walk with me.

No. 99.

1 Stand up!—stand up for Jesus!
　Ye soldiers of the cross;
Lift high His royal banner,
　It must not suffer loss:
From victory unto victory
　His army shall He lead,
Till every foe is vanquished,
　And Christ is Lord indeed.

2 Stand up!—stand up for Jesus!
　The trumpet call obey.
Forth to the mighty conflict,
　In this his glorious day:
"Ye that are men, now serve him,"
　Against unnumbered foes;
Let courage rise with danger,
　And strength to strength oppose

3 Stand up!—stand up for Jesus!
　Stand in His strength alone;
The arm of flesh will fail you—
　Ye dare not trust your own:
Put on the gospel armor,
　And, watching unto prayer,
Where duty calls, or danger,
　Be never wanting there.

4 Stand up!—stand up for Jesus!
　The strife will not be long;
This day, the noise of battle,
　The next, the victor's song:
To him that overcometh,
　A crown of life shall be;
He with the King of glory
　Shall reign eternally!
　　　　　　　　G. DUFFIELD.

No. 100.

1 To-day thy mercy calls me,
　To wash away my sin;
However great my trespass,
　Whate'er I may have been.
However long from mercy,
　I may have turned away,
Thy blood, O Christ! can cleanse me,
　And make me white to-day.

2 To-day thy gate is open,
　And all who enter in
Shall find a Father's welcome,
　And pardon for their sin;
The past shall be forgotten,
　A present joy be given,
A further grace be promised—
　A glorious crown in heaven.

3 To-day the Father calls me;
　The Holy Spirit waits;
The blessed angels gather
　Around the heavenly gates;
No question will be asked me
　How often I have come;
Altho' I oft have wandered,
　It is my Father's home.
　　　　　　　OSWALD ALLEN.

Hamburg. L M. Arr. by Dr. L. Mason.

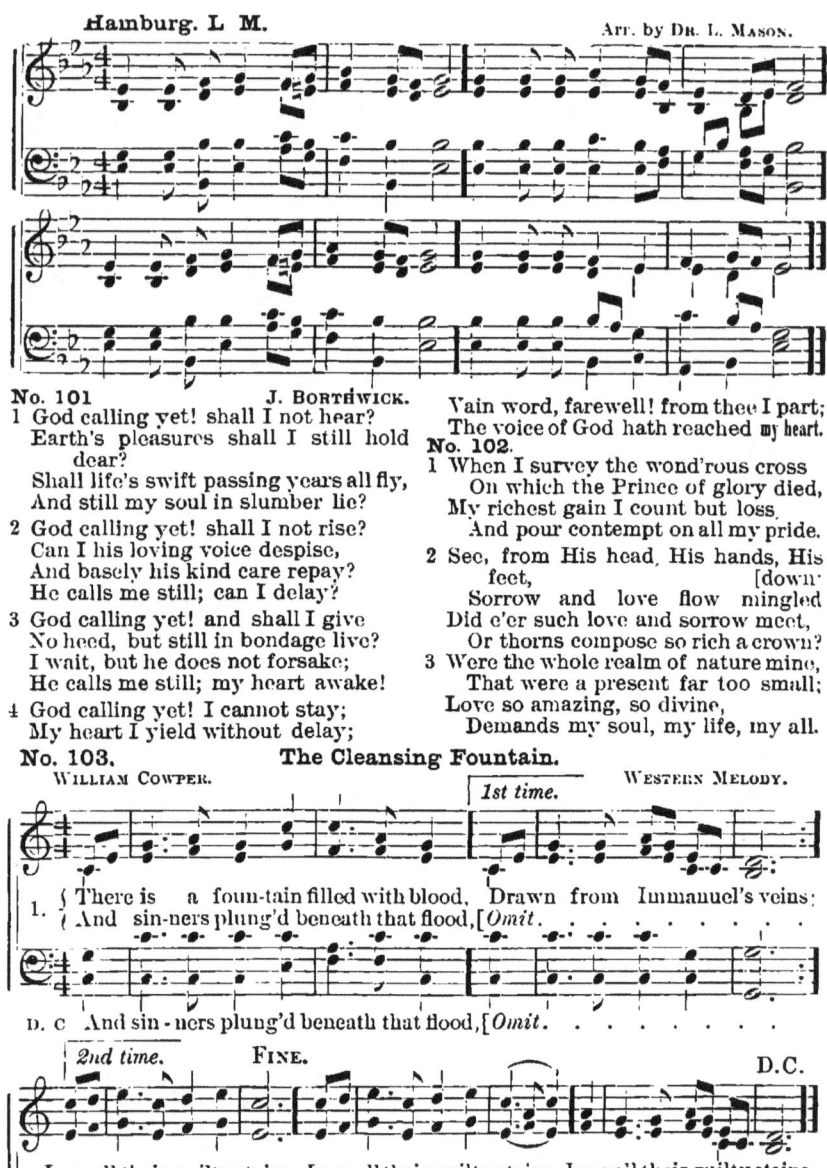

No. 101 J. Borthwick.
1 God calling yet! shall I not hear?
  Earth's pleasures shall I still hold dear?
  Shall life's swift passing years all fly,
  And still my soul in slumber lie?

2 God calling yet! shall I not rise?
  Can I his loving voice despise,
  And basely his kind care repay?
  He calls me still; can I delay?

3 God calling yet! and shall I give
  No heed, but still in bondage live?
  I wait, but he does not forsake;
  He calls me still; my heart awake!

4 God calling yet! I cannot stay;
  My heart I yield without delay;
  Vain word, farewell! from thee I part;
  The voice of God hath reached my heart.

No. 102.
1 When I survey the wond'rous cross
  On which the Prince of glory died,
  My richest gain I count but loss,
  And pour contempt on all my pride.

2 See, from His head, His hands, His feet,
  Sorrow and love flow mingled [down
  Did e'er such love and sorrow meet,
  Or thorns compose so rich a crown?

3 Were the whole realm of nature mine,
  That were a present far too small;
  Love so amazing, so divine,
  Demands my soul, my life, my all.

No. 103.   The Cleansing Fountain.
William Cowper.   Western Melody.

Pleyel's Hymn. 7.

No. 104.

1 Hasten, sinner, to be wise!
    Stay not for the morrow's sun:
Wisdom if you still despise
    Harder is it to be won.

2 Hasten, mercy to implore!
    Stay not for the morrow's sun:
Lest thy season should be o'er
    Ere this evening's stage be run.

3 Hasten, sinner, to return!
    Stay not for the morrow's sun
Lest thy lamp should fail to burn
    Ere salvation's work is done.

No. 105.

1 Hark! my soul, it is the Lord;
    'Tis Thy Saviour, hear His word;
Jesus speaks, and speaks to thee,
    "Say, poor sinner, lovest thou Me?"

2 "I delivered thee when bound,
    And when wounded, healed thy wound;
Sought thee wandering, set thee right,
    Turned thy darkness into light.

3 "Can a woman's tender care
    Cease towards the child she bare?
Yes, she may forgetful be;
    Yet will I remember thee.

4 "Mine is an unchanging love,
    Higher than the heights above.
Deeper than the depths beneath,
    Free and faithful, strong as death.

5 "Thou shalt see My glory soon
    When the work of grace is done;
Partner of My throne shalt be:
    Say, poor sinner, lovest thou Me?"

6 Lord, it is my chief complaint
    That my love is weak and faint;
Yet I love Thee, and adore:
    Oh for grace to love Thee more!

No. 106.

1 Take my life and let it be
    Consecrated, Lord to Thee,
Take my hands a d let them move
    At the impulse of Thy love.

2 Take my moments and my days,
    Let them flow in ceaseless praise;

Take my will and make it Thine,
    Let it be no longer mine.

3 Take my heart, it is Thine own,
    Let it be Thy royal throne,
Take, my love, my Lord I pour
    At Thy feet its treasures store.

No. 107.

1 People of the living God,
    I have sought the world around,
Paths of sin and sorrow trod,
    Peace and comfort nowhere found.

2 Now to you my spirit turns,
    Turns, a fugitive unblest;
Brethren, where your altar burns,
    Oh receive me into rest.

3 Lonely I no longer roam,
    Like the cloud, the wind, the wave;
Where you dwell shall be my home,
    Where you die shall be my grave.

4 Mine the God whom you adore,
    Your Redeemer shall be mine;
Earth can fill my heart no more,
    Every idol I resign.

No. 108.

1 Christ, of all my hopes the Ground,
    Christ the Spring of all my joy,
Still in thee let me be found,
    Still for Thee my powers employ.

2 Fountain of o'erflowing grace!
    Freely from Thy fullness give;
Till I close my earthly race,
    Be it "Christ for me to live!"

3 Firmly trusting in Thy blood,
    Nothing shall my heart confound;
Safely I shall pass the flood,
    Safely reach Immanuel's ground.

4 When I touch the blessed shore,
    Back the closing waves shall roll!
Death's dark stream shall nevermore
    Part from Thee my ravished soul.

5 Thus—oh, thus an entrance give
    To the land of cloudless sky;
Having known it "Christ to live,"
    Let me know it "gain to die."
                                R. WARDLAW.

Azmon. C. M.

No. 109.

1 Salvation! O the joyful sound!
   What pleasure to our ears;
   A sovereign balm for every wound,
   A cordial for our fears.

2 Salvation! let the echo fly
   The spacious earth around,
   While all the armies of the sky
   Conspire to raise the sound.

3 Salvation! O Thou bleeding Lamb!
   To Thee the praise belongs:
   Salvation shall inspire our hearts,
   And dwell upon our tongues.

No. 110.

1 Come, let us join our cheerful songs
   With angels round the throne;
   Ten thousand thousand are their
   But all their joys are one. [tongues,

2 "Worthy the Lamb that died," they
   "To be exalted thus!"   [cry,
   "Worthy the Lamb!" our lips reply,
   "For He was slain for us."

3 Jesus is worthy to receive
   Honor and power divine;   [give,
   And blessings, more than we can
   Be, Lord, for ever Thine!

4 Let all that dwell above the sky,
   And air, and earth, and seas,
   Conspire to lift Thy glories high,
   And speak Thine endless praise

5 The whole creation join in one,
   To bless the sacred name
   Of Him who sits upon the throne,
   And to adore the Lamb!
                       I. WATTS.

No. 111.

1 O, for a closer walk with God,
   A calm and heavenly frame;
   A light to shine upon the road
   That leads me to the Lamb!

2 Return, O Holy Dove, return,
   Sweet messenger of rest!
   I hate the sins that made thee mourn
   and drove thee from my breast.

3 The dearest idol I have known,
   What e'er that idol be,
   Help me to tear it from thy throne,
   And worship only thee.

4 So shall my walk be close with God,
   Calm and serene my frame;
   So purer light shall mark the road
   That leads me to the Lamb
                       W. COWPER.

No. 112.

1 How shall the young secure their
                      hearts,
   And guard their lives from sin?
   Thy word the choicest rules imparts
   To keep the conscience clean.

2 When once it enters to the mind,
   It spreads such light abroad,
   The meanest souls instruction find,
   And raise their thoughts to God.

3 'T is like the sun, a heavenly light,
   That guides us all the day;
   And through the dangers of the night
   A lamp to lead our way.

4 Thy precepts make me truly wise;
   I hate the sinner's road;
   I hate my own vain thoughts that
                      rise,
   But love thy law, my God!

5 Thy word is everlasting truth;
   How pure is every page!
   That holy book shall guide our youth,
   And well support our age.

Boylston. S. M.
LOWELL MASON.

No. 113

1 A charge to keep I have,
  A God to glorify,
A never-dying soul to save,
  And fit it for the sky.

2 To serve the present age,
  My calling to fulfill;
Oh, may it all my powers engage
  To do my Master's will.

3 Arm me with jealous care,
  As in thy sight to live;
And oh, thy servant, Lord, prepare
  A strict account to give.

4 Help me to watch and pray,
  And on thyself rely,
Assured, if I my trust betray,
  I shall for ever die.
            C. WESLEY.

No. 114.

1 My soul, be on thy guard,
  Ten thousand foes arise;
And hosts of sin are pressing hard
  To draw thee from the skies.

2 Oh, watch, and fight, and pray!
  The battle ne'er give o'er;
Renew it boldly every day,
  And help divine implore.

3 Ne'er think the victory won,
  Nor lay thine armour down;
Thine arduous work will not be done,
  Till thou obtain thy crown.

4 Fight on, my soul, till death
  Shall bring thee to thy God !
He'll take thee at thy parting breath,
  Up to his blest abode.
            G. HEATH.

No. 115.

1 I love thy kingdom, Lord,
  The house of thine abode,
The Church our blest Redeemer saved
  With His own precious blood.

2 I love thy Church, O God!
  Her walls before thee stand,
Dear as the apple of thine eye,
  And graven on thy hand.

3 For her my tears shall fall,
  For her my prayers ascend;
To her my cares and toils be given,
  Till toils and cares shall end.

4 Beyond my highest joy
  I prize her heavenly ways,
Her sweet communion, solemn vows,
  Her hymns of love and praise.

No. 116.

1 Now is the accepted time,
  Now is the day of grace;
O sinners! come, without delay,
  And seek the Saviour's face.

2 Now is the accepted time,
  The Saviour calls to day;
To-morrow it may be too late;—
  Then why should you delay?

3 Now is the accepted time,
  The gospel bids you come;
And every promise in his word
  Declares there yet is room.

4 Lord, draw reluctant souls,
  And feast them with thy love;
Then will the angels spread their wings,
  And bear the news above.

Duke Street. L. M.   John Hatton.

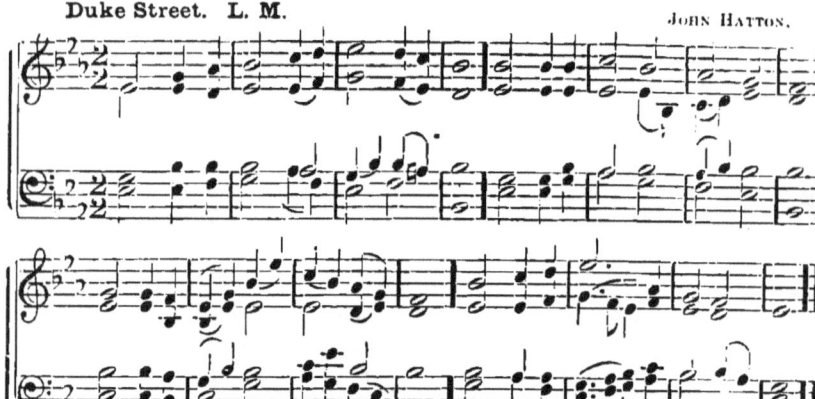

No. 117.

1 Lord, I am Thine, entirely Thine,
   Purchased and saved by blood divine,
  With full consent Thine I would be,
  And own Thy sovereign right in me.

2 Grant one poor sinner more a place
  Among the children of Thy grace;
  A wretched sinner, lost to God,
  But ransomed by Immanuel's blood.

3 Thine would I live, Thine would I die,
  Be Thine through all eternity;
  The vow is past beyond repeal;
  And now I set the solemn seal.

4 Here at that cross where flows the blood
  That bought my guilty soul for God,
  Thee, my new Master now I call,
  And consecrate to Thee my all.

No. 118.

1 Jesus shall reign where'er the sun
  Does his successive journeys run;
  His kingdom spread from shore to shore,
  Till moons shall wax and wane no more.

2 From north to south the princes meet,
  To pay their homage at His feet;
  While western empires own their Lord,
  And savage tribes attend His word.

3 To Him shall endless prayer be made,
  And endless praises crown His head;
  His name like sweet perfume shall rise
  With every morning sacrifice.
                Scottish Tune.

No. 119.

1 So let our lips and lives express
  The holy gospel we profess;
  So let our works and virtues shine,
  To prove the doctrine all divine.

2 Thus shall we best proclaim abroad
  The honors of our Saviour God;
  When His salvation reigns within,
  And grace subdues the power of sin.

3 Religion bears our spirits up,
  While we expect that blessed hope,—
  The bright appearance of the Lord:
  And faith stands leaning on His word.
                Rev. I. Watts.

No. 120.

1 Now I resolve with all my heart,
  With all my powers to serve the Lord;
  Nor from His precepts e'er depart,
  Whose service is a rich reward.

2 Oh! be His service all my joy!—
  Around let my example shine,
  Till others love the blest employ,
  And join in labors so divine.

3 Be this the purpose of my soul,
  My solemn, my determined choice,
  To yield to His supreme control,
  And, in His kind commands, rejoice.

4 Oh! may I never faint nor tire,
  Nor wandering leave His sacred ways,
  Great God! accept my soul's desire,
  And give me strength to live Thy praise.
                Annie Steele.

Avon C. M.
Scottisch Tune.

No. 121.

1. O for a heart to praise my God,
   A heart from sin set free!
   A heart that always feels thy blood,
   So freely spilt for me!

2. A heart resigned, submissive, meek,
   My great Redeemer's throne;
   Where only Christ is heard to speak;
   Where Jesus reigns alone.

3. O for a lowly, contrite heart,
   Believing, true, and clean,
   Which neither life nor death can part
   From him that dwells within!

4. A heart in every thought renewed,
   And full of love divine;
   Perfect and right, and pure, and good,
   A copy, Lord, of thine.

No. 122.

1. O for a faith that will not shrink,
   Though pressed by every foe,
   That will not tremble on the brink
   Of any earthly woe!

2. A faith that shines more bright and clear
   When tempests rage without;
   That when in danger knows no fear,
   In darkness feels no doubt;

3. A faith that keeps the narrow way
   Till life's last hour is fled,
   And with a pure and heavenly ray
   Illumes a dying bed.

4. Lord, give us such a faith as this,
   And then, whate'er may come,
   We'll taste, e'en here, the hallowed bliss
   Of an eternal home.

No. 123. My Faith Looks up to Thee.
L. Mason.

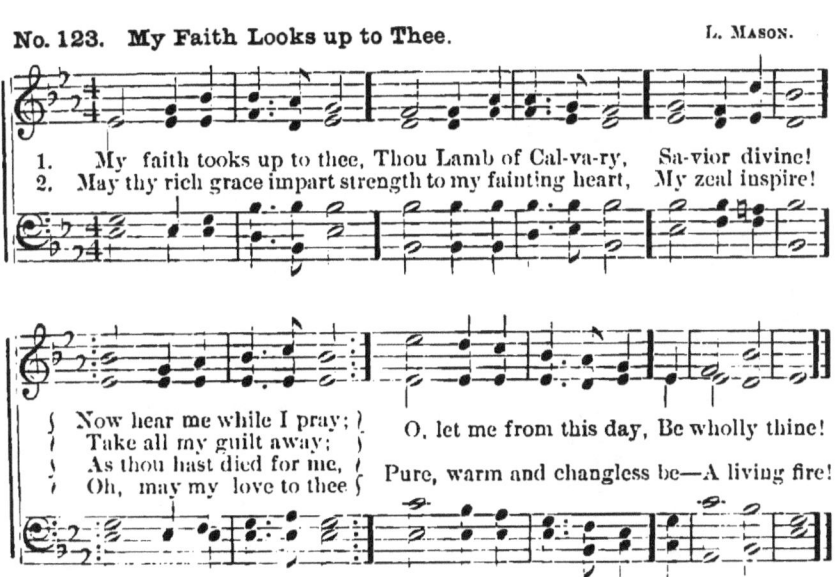

3. While life's dark maze I tread,
   And griefs around me spread,
   Be Thou my guide;
   Bid darkness turn to-day,
   Wipe sorrow's tears away,
   Nor let me ever stray
   From Thee aside.

4. When ends life's transient dream,
   When death's cold, sullen stream
   Shall o'er me roll,
   Blest Saviour! then, in love,
   Fear and distrust remove;
   Oh, bear me safe above—
   A ransomed soul!

Hamburg. L. M. Arr. by Dr. L. Mason.

No. 124.

1 Just as I am, without one plea,
  But that thy blood was shed for me,
  And that thou bid'st me come to thee
   O Lamb of God, I come!

2 Just as I am, and waiting not
  To rid my soul of one dark blot,
  To thee whose blood can cleanse each spot,
   O Lamb of God, I come!

3 Just as I am, though tossed about
  With many a conflict, many a doubt,
  Fightings within, and fears without.
   O Lamb of God, I come!

4 Just as I am—thou wilt receive,
  Wilt welcome, pardon, cleanse, relieve;
  Because thy promise I believe,
   O Lamb of God, I come!

5 Just as I am—thy love unknown
  Hath broken every barrier down;
  Now, to be thine, yea, thine alone.
   O, Lamb of God, I come!

No. 125.

1 With tearful eyes I look around;
   Life seems a dark and stormy sea;
  Yet, 'mid the gloom, I hear a sound,
   A heavenly whisper, "Come to me."

2 It tells me of a place of rest—
   It tells me where my soul may flee;
  O! to the weary, faint, oppressed [me.
   How sweet the bidding, 'Come to

3 When nature shudders, loath to part
   From all I love, enjoy, and see;
  When a faint chill steals o'er my heart,
   A sweet voice utters, "Come to me."

4 Come, for all else must fail and die;
  Earth is no resting-place for thee;
  Heavenward direct thy weeping eye,
   I am thy portion! "Come to me."

5 O voice of mercy! voice of love!
   In conflict, grief and agony,
  Support me, cheer me from above,
   And gently whisper, "Come to me.'

No. 126.

1 My God, my Father, while I stray
  Far from my home on life's rough way
  O teach me from my heart to say,
   "Thy will be done! Thy will be done!"

2 What though in lonely grief I sigh;
  For friends beloved no longer nigh;
  Submissive still would I reply,
   "Thy will be done! Thy will be done!"

3 If thou shouldst call me to resign
  What most I prize,—it ne'er was mine;
  I only yield thee what was thine;
   "Thy will be done! Thy will be done!"

4 If but my fainting heart be blest
  With thy sweet Spirit for its guest,
  My God, to thee I leave the rest:
   "Thy will be done! Thy will be done!"

5 Renew my will from day to day;
  Blend it with thine, and take away
  Whate'er now makes it hard to say,
   "Thy will be done! Thy will be done!"

6 Then when on earth I breathe no more
  The prayer oft mixed with tears before
  I'll sing upon a happier shore:
   "Thy will be done! Thy will be done!"

No. 127. O Happy Day.

PHILIP DODDRIDGE. English Melody.

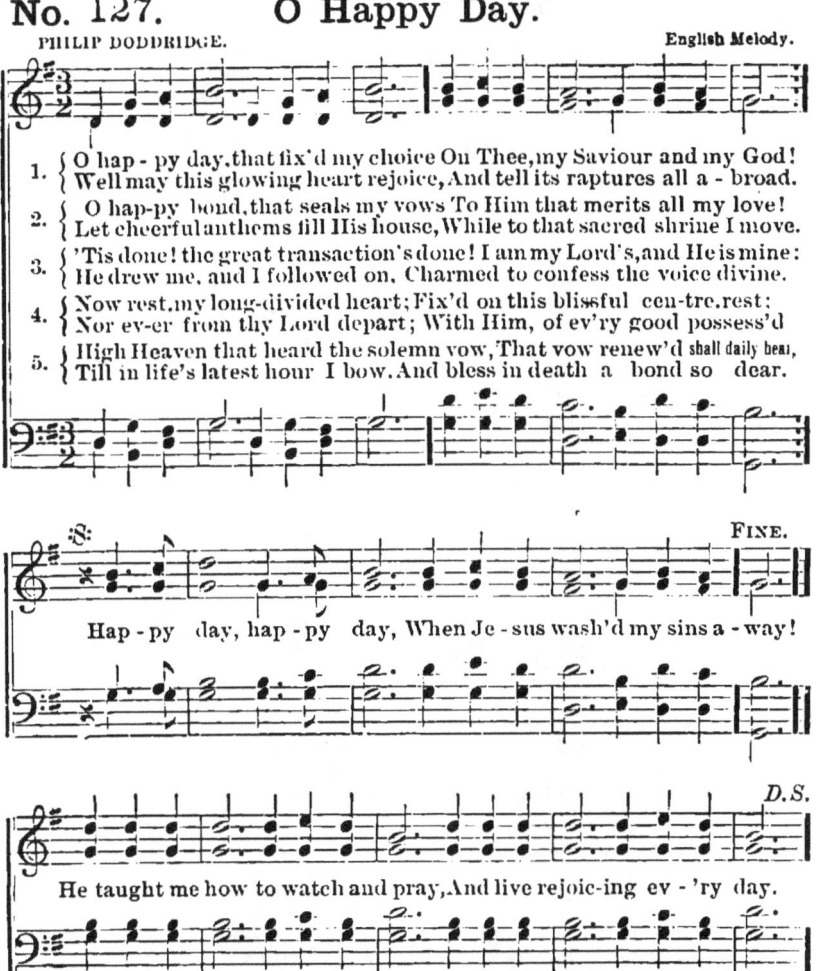

1. O hap-py day, that fix'd my choice On Thee, my Saviour and my God!
   Well may this glowing heart rejoice, And tell its raptures all a-broad.
2. O hap-py bond, that seals my vows To Him that merits all my love!
   Let cheerful anthems fill His house, While to that sacred shrine I move.
3. 'Tis done! the great transaction's done! I am my Lord's, and He is mine;
   He drew me, and I followed on, Charmed to confess the voice divine.
4. Now rest, my long-divided heart; Fix'd on this blissful cen-tre, rest;
   Nor ev-er from thy Lord depart; With Him, of ev'ry good possess'd
5. High Heaven that heard the solemn vow, That vow renew'd shall daily hear,
   Till in life's latest hour I bow, And bless in death a bond so dear.

Hap-py day, hap-py day, When Je-sus wash'd my sins a-way!

He taught me how to watch and pray, And live rejoic-ing ev-'ry day.

No. 128.

1 I have a Saviour, He's pleading in glory, [friends be few;
   A dear, loving Saviour, tho' earth
   And now He is watching in tender-
   [ness o'er me, [Saviour too.
   And oh, that my Saviour were your
       For you I am praying,
       For you I am praying,
       For you I am praying,
       I am praying for you.

2 I have a Father: to me he has given
   A hope for eternity, blessed and true;
   And soon will He call me to meet
       Him in heaven, [with me too!
   But oh, that He'd let me bring you

3 I have a robe: 'tis resplendent in
       whiteness, [view;
   Awaiting in glory my wondering

   Oh, when I receive it all shining in
       brightness,
   Dear friends, could I see you receiv-
       ing one too!

4 I have a peace: it is calm as a river,—
   A peace that the friends of this world
       never knew; [Giver,
   My Saviour alone is its Author and
   And oh, could I know it was given to
       you!

5 When Jesus has found you, tell others
       the story, [Saviour too;
   That my loving Saviour is your
   Then pray that your Saviour may
       bring them to glory,
   And prayer will be answered, 'twas
       answered for you!

Martyn. 7s. Double.

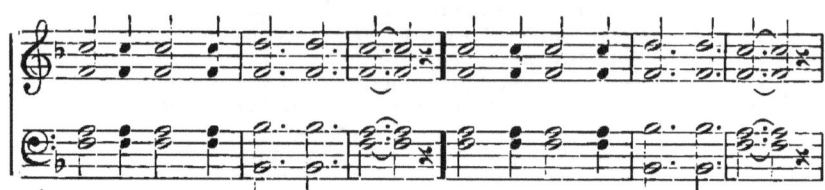

No. 129.

1 Sinners, turn, why will ye die?
God, your Maker, asks you why?
God, who did your being give,
Made you with himself to live;
He the fatal cause demands,
Asks the work of his own hands—
Why, ye thankless creatures, why
Will ye cross his love, and die?

2 Sinners, turn, why will ye die?
God, your Saviour asks you why?
He who did your souls retrieve,
Died himself, that ye might live.
Will ye let him die in vain?
Crucify your Lord again?
Why, ye ransomed sinners, why
Will ye slight his grace, and die?

3 Sinners, turn, why will ye die?
God, the Spirit, asks you why?
He, who all your lives hath strove
Urged you to embrace his love.
Will ye not his grace receive?
Will ye still refuse to live?
O ye dying sinners! why—
Why will ye forever die?

No. 130.

1 Jesus! lover of my soul,
  Let me to thy bosom fly
While the billows near me roll,
  While the tempest still is high;
Hide me, O my Saviour! hide,
  Till the storm of life is past;
Safe into the haven guide;
  Oh, receive my soul at last!

2 Other refuge have I none;
  Hangs my helpless soul on thee;
Leave, ah! leave me not alone,
  Still support and comfort me.
All my trust on thee is stayed;
  All my help from thee I bring;
Cover my defenceless head
  With the shadow of thy wing.

3 Plenteous grace with thee is found,
  Grace to pardon all my sin;
Let the healing streams abound,
  Make and keep me pure within;
Thou of life the fountain art,
  Freely let me take of thee;
Spring thou up within my heart,
  Rise to all eternity.   C. WESLEY.

Greenville. 8s, 7s, 4s. J. J. Rousseau.

No. 131.

1 Jesus, I my cross have taken,
　All to leave, and follow thee;
　Naked, poor, despised, forsaken,
　　Thou, from hence, my all shalt be!
　Perish, every fond ambition,
　All I've sought, or hoped, or known,
　Yet how rich is my condition,
　　God and heaven are still my own!

2 Let the world despise and leave me,
　They have left my Saviour, too;
　Human hearts and looks deceive me—
　　Thou art not, like them, untrue;
　Oh, while thou dost smile upon me,
　God of wisdom, love and might,
　Foes may hate and friends disown me,
　　Show thy face, and all is bright.

3 Man may trouble and distress me,
　'Twill but drive me to thy breast;
　Life with trials hard may press me;
　　Heaven will bring me sweeter rest!
　Oh, 'tis not in grief to harm me,
　While thy love is left to me;
　Oh, 'twere not in joy to charm me,
　　Were that joy unmixed with thee.

4 Go then, earthly fame and treasure!
　Come, disaster, scorn, and pain!
　In thy service pain is pleasure,
　　With thy favor loss is gain.
　I have called thee—Abba, Father!
　I have stayed my heart on thee!
　Storms may howl, and clouds may gather,
　　All must work for good to me.
　　　　　　　　　　　　H. F. LYTE.

No. 132.

1 Come, ye sinners, poor and wretched,
　Weak and wounded, sick and sore
　Jesus ready stands to save you,
　　Full of pity, love and power,
　　　He is able,
　He is willing, doubt no more.

2 Ho, ye needy; come, and welcome;
　God's free bounty glorify!
　True belief and true repentance,
　　Every grace that brings us nigh,
　　　Without money,
　Come to Jesus Christ, and buy.

3 Let not conscience make you linger,
　Nor of fitness fondly dream;
　All the fitness he requireth
　　Is to feel your need of him;
　　　This he gives you;
　'Tis the Spirit's rising beam.
　　　　　　　　　　　　J. HART.

No 133.

1 Love divine, all love excelling,—
　Joy of heaven, to earth come down!
　Fix in us thy humble dwelling,
　　All thy faithful mercies crown;
　Jesus! thou art all compassion.
　Pure, unbounded love thou art;
　Visit us with thy salvation,
　Enter every trembling heart.

2 Breathe, oh, breathe thy loving Spirit
　Into every troubled breast!
　Let us all in thee inherit,
　　Let us find the promised rest·
　Come, Almighty, to deliver,
　Let us all thy life receive!
　Speedily return, and never,
　Never more thy temples leave!

3 Finish, then, then thy new creation,
　Pure, unspotted may we be:
　Let us see our whole salvation
　　Perfectly secured by thee!
　Changed from glory into glory,
　Till in heaven we take our place;
　Till we cast our crowns before thee,
　Lost in wonder, love and praise.
　　　　　　　　　　　　C. WESLEY.

Expostulation. 11. J. HOPKINS.

No. 134.
1 Oh, turn ye, Oh, turn ye, for why will ye die, [so nigh?
When God, in great mercy, is coming
Now Jesus invites you, the Spirit says, come, [you home.
And angels are waiting to welcome

2 In riches, in pleasures, what can you obtain, [your pain?
To soothe your affliction, or banish
To bear up your spirit, when summoned to die, [high?
Or waft you to mansions of glory on

3 And now Christ is ready your souls to receive,]believe?
Oh, how can you question if you will
If sin is your burden, why will you not come? [you come home.
'Tis you He bids welcome; He bids
J. HOPKINS.

No. 135.
1 Acquaint thyself quickly, O sinner, with God, [beam on thy road,
And joy, like the sunshine, shall
And peace, like the dew drop, shall fall on thy head, [thy bed.
And sleep, like an angel, shall visit

2 Acquaint thyself quickly, O sinner, with God, [fears are abroad.
And he shall be with thee when
Thy Safeguard in danger that threatens thy path; [death;
Thy joy in the valley and shadow of
KNOX.

No 136.
1 Delay not, delay not, O sinner, draw near,
The waters of life are now flowing for thee;
No price is demanded, the Saviour is here; [free.
Redemption is purchased, salvation is

2 Delay not, delay not, O sinner, to come, [thee to-day:
For Mercy still lingers, and calls
Her voice is not heard in the vale of the tomb; [pass away.
Her message, unheeded, will soon

3 Delay not, delay not, the Spirit of grace [take his sad flight,
Long grieved and resisted may
And leave thee in darkness to finish thy race, [night.
To sink in the gloom of eternity's
T. HASTINGS.

No. 137.
1 To-day the Saviour calls;
Ye wand'rers come;
O, ye benighted souls,
Why longer roam?

2 To-day the Saviour calls:
O, listen now;
Within these sacred walls
To Jesus bow.

3 To-day the Saviour calls:
For refuge fly;
The storm of justice falls,
And death is nigh.

4 The Spirit calls to-day.
Yield to His power;
O, grieve Him not away;
'Tis mercy's hour.

o. 138.

How firm a foundation, ye saints of
   the Lord!   [word.
Is laid for your faith in his excellent
What more can he say, than to you
   he hath said,—   [fled?
To you, who for refuge to Jesus have
"Fear not, I am with thee, oh, be not
   dismayed,   [thee aid;
For I am thy God, I will still give
I'll strengthen thee, help thee, and
   cause thee to stand,   [hand.
Upheld by my gracious, omnipotent
"When through the deep waters I
   call thee to go,   [flow.
The rivers of sorrow shall not over-
For I will be with thee thy trouble to
   bless.   [tress.
And sanctify to thee thy deepest dis-
The soul that on Jesus hath leaned
   for repose,
I will not I will not desert to his foes;
That soul — though all hell should
   endeavor to shake,   [sake."
I'll never—no never—no never for-

o. 139.

The Lord is my Shepherd, no want
   shall I know;   [I rest;
I feed in green pastures, safe-folded
He leadeth my soul where the still
   waters flow,
Restores me when wandering, re-
   deems when oppressed.
Through the valley and shadow of
   death though I stray.   [fear;
Since thou art my Guardian no evil I

Thy rod shall defend me, thy staff be
   my stay;   [forter near.
No harm can befall, with my Com-
3 In the midst of affliction, my table
   is spread;   [cup runneth o'er;
With blessings unmeasured, my
With perfume and oil thou anointest
   my head;   [dence more?
Oh, what shall I ask of thy provi-
4 Let goodness and mercy, my bountiful God!   [above;
Still follow my steps till I meet thee
I seek, by the path which my fore-
   fathers trod
Through the land of their sojourn,
   thy kingdom of love.
                      J. MONTGOMERY.

No. 140.

1 I once was a stranger to grace and to
   God;   [my loud.
I knew not my danger, and felt not
Though friends spoke in rapture of
   Christ on the tree,   [to me.
Jehovah, my Savior, seemed nothing
2 When free grace awoke me by light
   from on high,   [to die.
Then legal fears shook me; I trembled
No refuge, no safety, in self could I
   see: [be!
Jehovah, thou only my Saviour must
3 My terrors all vanished before his
   sweet name;   [ness I came
My guilty fears banished, with bold-
To drink at the fountain so copious
   and free: [to me.
Jehovah, my Saviour, is all things
                      R. M. McCHEYNE.

1 Come unto me, when shadows darkly
    gather,   [distressed;
  When the sad heart is weary and
  Seeking for comfort from your heav-
    enly Father   [rest.
  Come unto me, and I will give you

2 Large are the mansions in thy father's
    dwelling,   [dim.
  Glad are the homes that sorrows never

  Sweet are the harps in holy mu
    swelling,   [heavenly hyr
  Soft are the tones which raise

3 There, like an Eden, blossoming
    gladness   [rudely press
  Bloom the fair flowers the earth
  Come unto me, all ye who droop
    sadness,   [re
  Come unto me, and I will give

Come ye disconsolate.

No. 142.

1 Come, ye disconsolate, wherever ye
    languish: [kneel;
  Come to the mercy seat, fervently
  Here bring your wounded hearts,
    here tell your anguish;
  Earth has no sorrow that heaven
    cannot heal.

2 Joy of the desolate, light of the
    straying,   [pure.
  Hope of the penitent, fadeless and

  Here speaks the Comforter, tende
    saying,
  Earth has no sorrow that hea
    cannot cure.

3 Here see the bread of life;
    waters flowing   [from abo
  Forth from the throne of God, p
  Come to the feast of love: come, e
    knowing   [remo
  Earth has no sorrow but heaven

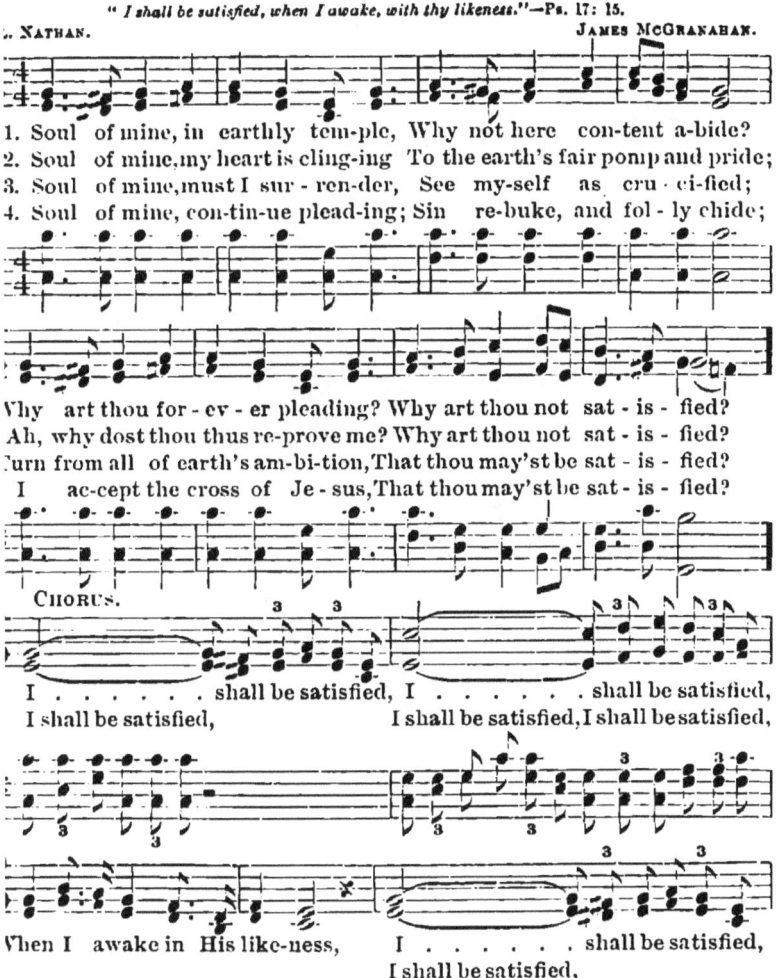

No 144. Depth of Mercy.

"God is Love."—1st John, 4:8.

CHARLES WESLEY. From Stevenson

1. Depth of mer-cy! can there be Mer-cy still re-served for r
   Can my God His wrath for-bear? Me, the chief of sinners, spa
2. I have long withstood His grace, Long pro-voked Him to His fa
   Would not hearken to His calls; Grieved Him by a thousand f
3. Now in-cline me to re-pent; Let me now my sins lamen
   Now my foul re-volt de-plore, Weep, be-lieve, and sin no mo

CHORUS.

God is love! I know, I feel; Je-sus, lives, and loves me stil

Je-sus lives, He lives, and loves me still.

No. 145.

1 Yield not to temptation,
  For yielding is sin;
Each vict'ry will help you
  Some other to win;
Fight manfully onward,
  Dark passions subdue,
Look ever to Jesus,
  He'll carry you through.
CHO.—Ask the Savior to help you,
    Comfort, strengthen, and keep you,
    He is willing to aid you,
    He will carry you through

2 Shun evil companions,
  Bad language disdain,

God's name hold in reverence,
  Nor take it in vain;
Be thoughtful and earnest,
  Kind hearted and true,
Look ever to Jesus,
  He'll carry you through.—CHO

3 To him that o'ercometh,
  God giveth a crown,
Through faith we shall conquer,
  Though often cast down;
He who is your Saviour,
  Our strength will renew;
Look ever to Jesus,
  He'll carry you through.—CHO

No. 146. Jesus is Mine.

"My beloved is mine."—Song of Solomon 2:16.

Mrs. Catherine J. Bonar, 1843.   T. E. Perkins, by per.

1. Fade, fade each earth-ly joy, Jesus is mine! Break ev-ery tender tie, Jesus is mine! Dark is the wil-der-ness, Earth has no rest-ing place, Jesus a-lone can bless, Je-sus is mine.
2. Tempt not my soul a-way, Jesus is mine! Here would I ever stay, Jesus is mine! Per-ish-ing things of clay, Born but for one brief day, Pass from my heart away, Je-sus is mine.
3. Fare-well ye dreams of night, Jesus is mine! Lost in this dawn-ing light, Jesus is mine! All that my soul has tried Left but a dis-mal void, Je-sus has sat-is-fied, Je-sus is mine.
4. Fare-well mor-tal-i-ty, Jesus is mine! Wel-come e-ter-ni-ty, Jesus is mine! Welcome, O loved and blest Welcome, sweet scenes of rest, Welcome, my Savior's breast, Je-sus is mine.

No. 147.

1 Saviour! I follow on,
　Guided by thee,
　Seeing not yet the hand
　　That leadeth me:
Hushed be my heart and still,
Fear I no further ill;
Only to meet thy will
　My will shall be.

2 Riven the rock for me
　Thirst to relieve,
　Manna from heaven falls
　　Fresh every eve;
Never a want severe
Causeth my eye a tear,
But thou dost whisper near,
　"Only believe!"

3 Often to Marah's brink
　Have I been brought;
　Shrinking the cup to drink,
　　Help I have sought;
And with the prayer's ascent,
Jesus the branch hath rent—
Quickly relief hath sent.
　Sweetening the draught.

4 Saviour! I long to walk
　Closer with thee;
　Led by thy guiding hand,
　　Ever to be;
Constantly near thy side,
Quickened and purified,
Living for him who died
　Freely for me!

St. Thomas. S. M.

No. 148.
1 O Holy Spirit, come,
  And Jesus' love declare;
  O tell us of our heavenly home,
  And guide us safely there.

2 Our unbelief remove,
  By thine almighty breath;
  O work the wondrous work of love,
  The mighty work of faith.

3 Come with resistless power,
  Come with almighty grace,
  Come with the long expected show'r
  And fall upon this place.

No. 149.
1 O Lord, thy work revive,
  In Zion's gloomy hour,
  And let our dying graces live,
  By thy restoring power.

2 O let thy chosen few,
  Awake to earnest prayer;
  Their covenant again renew,
  And walk in filial fear.

3 Thy Spirit then will speak
  Thro' lips of humble clay,
  Till hearts of adamant shall break,
  Till rebels shall obey.

Brattle Street: C: M: D: I. PLEYEL.

No. 150.
1 While thee I seek, protecting power!
  Be my vain wishes stilled;
  And may this consecrated hour
  With better hopes be filled:
  Thy love the power of thought bestowed;
  To thee my thoughts would soar:
  Thy mercy o'er my life has flowed·
  That mercy I adore.

2 In each event of life how clear
  Thy ruling hand I see!
  Each blessing to my soul more dear
  Because conferred by thee.

In every joy that crowns my days,
  In every pain I bear.
  My heart shall find delight in praise
  Or seek relief in prayer.

3 When gladness wings my favored hour,
  Thy love my thoughts shall fill;
  Resigned, when storms of sorrow lower,
  My soul shall meet thy will.
  My lifted eye, without a tear,
  The gathering storm shall see;
  My steadfast heart shall know no fear;
  That heart will rest on thee.
                              H. M. WILLIAMS.

No. 151. The Saint's Home. 11.

HENRY ROWLEY BISHOP.

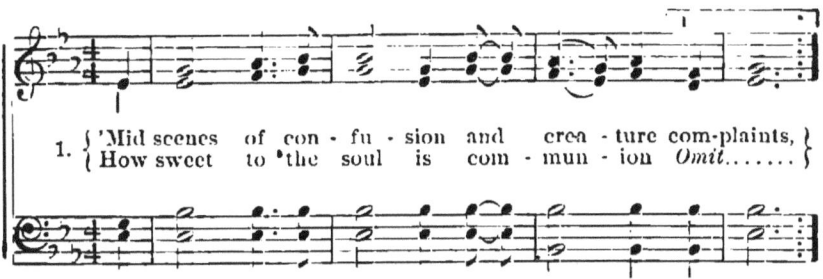

1. 'Mid scenes of con-fu-sion and crea-ture com-plaints,
   How sweet to the soul is com-mun-ion *Omit.......*

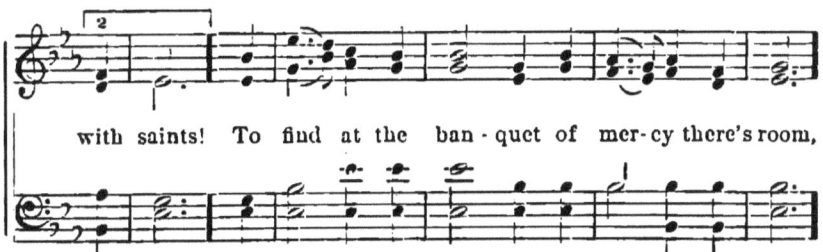

with saints! To find at the ban-quet of mer-cy there's room,

And feel in the presence of Jesus at home. Home! home! sweet, sweet home!
D.S. Prepare me, dear Savior, for glory, my home.

2 Sweet bonds that unite all the children of peace!
And, thrice precious Jesus, whose love cannot cease,
Tho' oft from thy presence in sadness I roam,
I long to behold thee in glory at home

3 I sigh from this body of sin to be free, [munion with thee;
Which hinders my joy and com-
Tho' now my temptation like billows may foam,
All, all will be peace when I'm with thee at home.

4 While here in the valley of conflict I stay,
O give me submission, and strength as my day;
In all my afflictions to thee would I come, [home.
Rejoicing in hope of my glorious

5 I long, dearest Lord, in thy beauties to shine; [pine.
No more as an exile in sorrow to
And in thy dear image arise from the tomb,
With glorified millions to praise thee at home;

DAVID DENHAM.

www.ingramcontent.com/pod-product-compliance
Lightning Source LLC
Chambersburg PA
CBHW031606110426
42742CB00037B/1301